Mr. STEIN

A Biography of
JOCK STEIN C.B.E. 1922-85

Bob Crampsey

MAINSTREAM
PUBLISHING

First published in 1986 by
MAINSTREAM PUBLISHING COMPANY (EDINBURGH), LTD.
7 Albany Street
Edinburgh EH1 3UG

ISBN 1 85158 057 3 (cased)
ISBN 1 85158 058 1 (P/back)

Typeset by Pulse Origination, Edinburgh.
Printed in Great Britain by by Billing & Sons Ltd, Worcester.

CONTENTS

ACKNOWLEDGEMENTS

MANY very busy people made time to talk to me in the course of the preparation of this book. Sean Fallon allowed me to draw freely on his long experience of Jock Stein as playing and working colleague. Of those who played for him Jim Craig, John Cushley and Danny McGrain were most helpful in describing what it was like to be one of the Celtic first-team squad under Stein.

Jack McGinn, originator of the *Celtic View* and present chairman of the Board of Celtic FC was unfailingly courteous and helpful in confirming and sometimes dispelling impressions. Of the many players who found themselves pitted against Stein at club level I am most indebted to Alan Rough of Partick Thistle, Hibernian and Scotland and to Alan Gordon who played with distinction for the two Edinburgh sides and Dundee United.

Harry Andrew of the *Sunday Express*, that most graceful writer, drew on an acquaintanceship of thirty years or more and very valuable individual perceptions were contributed by former FIFA referee R. H. Davidson and by Jimmy Gordon, maker of the film *The Celtic Story* and currently managing director of Radio Clyde. Walter McCrae of Kilmarnock FC provided an invaluable insight into Stein's early days as manager of Scotland and of the travails which beset a manager of a professional football club. In the very last stages of preparation Andy Roxburgh, newly-appointed to take charge of the Scotland side, told me something of what he had learned under Stein's tutelage.

Many others were also extremely kind with their generous provision of source material. I would particularly mention Bobby Kerr and Robin Marwick who furnished me with excellent material on the Albion Rovers period, Douglas Scott who passed on to me some very useful information on the Dunfermline days and Pat Woods who was generosity itself in supplying material from his unrivalled collection of Celtic memorabilia, to say nothing of his contribution in the way of meticulous checking. The Rev. Dr James Martin of Carntyne High Parish Church, Glasgow, kindly let me have the text of the funeral service for Jock Stein.

To all the above mentioned gentlemen I am heavily obigated but of course the views expressed in the book are my own and none of those mentioned above would necessarily identify themselves with them. I have tried not only to describe a career in detail but to analyse those characteristics of the man which made Jock Stein such an astonishing success in his chosen life's work. There may be other views and I happily leave it to the reader to assess my own success or failure in this attempt to reveal a very private public man.

THE LAST DAY

THE mood of the Scottish supporters who thronged into Cardiff in the dawn hours of 10 September 1985 was markedly different from that of those fans who had attended the corresponding match against Wales at Anfield eight years before. In 1977 there had been a thoroughly unhealthy kind of hysteria, a determination on the terracings to qualify by fair means or foul and it is now history that Scotland qualified by dubious means which attracted instant and humiliating retribution.

Cardiff, 1985, was another matter. The atmosphere was one of hope rather than of expectation. It seemed as if it would be 1965 all over again, with a good start in the qualifying section of the World Cup dissipated by an unexpected home defeat. Then it had been Poland, this time Wales themselves. Defeat in Spain had been by the narrowest margin possible but it was still defeat and the performance against Iceland in Reykjavik had been abysmal. Outplayed, out-thought, the Scotland side had scraped through thanks to the generosity of their hosts whose prodigality stretched to a missed penalty kick. In that game Jock Stein's gnawing anxiety had surfaced when he attacked the referee for delaying a long time before making up his mind to book Graeme Souness. Most objective observers thought the Scots captain was lucky to stay on the field considering the severity of his tackle on the young Icelandic forward Sigi Jonsson.

That was all in the past. Now on this early September day Scotland had at least to draw the match with Wales to go into a two-match play-off with the winners of the Australian section. The Welsh had already won at Hampden and won well. In addition they possessed two proven strikers in Ian Rush of Liverpool and Mark Hughes of Manchester United. Even with the knowledge that Scotland only needed to draw, most people would have thought there was a shade of odds in favour of Wales, and certainly, with their very survival as a separate footballing entity at stake, the Welsh would not lack in effort.

Some prominent Scots players would be missing. Souness was under suspension and Stein learned from Terry Venables of Barcelona that a combination of 'flu and an ankle knock would mean that Steve

Archibald would not travel from Spain. The loss of Souness was grievous but potentially even more damaging was the absence of the two Liverpool players, Alan Hansen and Kenny Dalglish.

None of this daunted the Scots fans who strolled around Cardiff shirtless on one of the pleasant days of an abominable summer. The massive police presence remained at a distance, unobtrusive, unrequired. Ian Rush was holding a signing session for his autobiography at a city bookstore and there was some good-humoured jibing from the *descamisados*, but nobody took it ill.

The Scots party had their headquarters in Bristol where Alex Ferguson had taken the training sessions while Stein had individual words with individual players. He was a little bit apprehensive that David Speedie, the Chelsea player, might become physically embroiled in his anxiety to do well so his talk with the player was directed to ensuring that he would channel his enthusiasm in the proper way.

There was the inevitable build-up of tension in the course of the day, something which never left him and something on which he used to say he thrived. Then, all preparations over, the teams took the field before a crowd in which the Scots were abundantly represented. Months of careful planning could be undone over the next ninety minutes by individual error. The teams lined up as follows:

> *Wales*: Southall (Everton); Jones (Huddersfield), Jackett (Watford), Ratcliffe, Van den Hauwe (Everton), Phillips (Manchester City), James (Queen's Park Rangers), Nicholas (Luton Town), Rush (Liverpool), Thomas (Chelsea), Hughes (Manchester United).
> *Scotland*: Leighton (Aberdeen); Gough, Malpas (Dundee United), Aitken (Celtic), McLeish, Miller (Aberdeen), Strachan (Manchester United), Nicol (Liverpool), Sharp (Everton), Bett (Aberdeen), Speedie (Chelsea).

The manager's very last involvement with the Scottish fans was humorous and amiable. There was no "Welsh end" or "Scottish end", largely because many of the Welsh tickets had gone to Scots. During shooting-in practice before kick-off, the Scots had refused to return those balls which had been kicked into the crowd. Neville Southall, the Welsh goalkeeper, enlisted the aid of the manager to secure the return. The gigantic figure walked heavily downfield and, with his hands, described the shape of a ball to the fans. A missing ball came flying out, then another. Southall indicated to Stein that there was a third but the latter seemed to suggest that two out of three was not bad going from a Scottish crowd. The little bit of by-play ended with Jock Stein, arm round the Welsh keeper's neck, having a friendly word as the teams changed over.

The game began badly with the Scottish side nervous and quite a few signs that the referee would be inconsistent. Within the first few minutes

Alex McLeish had been booked while a hefty challenge by Mark Hughes on the same player had gone unrecorded. Worse, the same Hughes put Wales ahead after 13 minutes, driving in a pass from Phillips on the left with all the assurance of a man hammering home a nail. From now on the Scots would struggle. Nicol was ill at ease and the normally composed Jim Leighton was causing palpitations by his erratic handling of the ball. The Welsh strike force of Rush and Hughes threatened to augment the Welsh lead while Micky Thomas, small, dark and looking like every Welsh scrum-half who ever played along the road at the Arms Park, buzzed about to great effect. Leighton came out for a cross-ball, lost it and was relieved to see the Scots defence scramble it clear. Just before half-time he allowed a harmless bouncing ball to escape him and only a courageous smother and a loss of nerve by the Welsh forward retrieved the situation. Half-time came with Scotland a goal down, short of attacking ideas, their fans gloomy.

That gloom was intensified when it was seen that there had been a dramatic change of goalkeepers at the start of the second half. Attention had been focused on the outfield players for a substitution there was not unlooked for, not uncalled for, some fans would have said, but there was Alan Rough taking his place between the Scottish posts. It emerged that Jim Leighton's unconvincing first-half display owed everything to his having lost a contact lens. It also emerged that he had left his spare lenses in the hotel at Bristol and that Stein had decided, after making his views felt, that a change of goalkeeper would have to be made. This drastically reduced his options. He now had one outfield change only that he could make and he would have to get it right.

Two things were to save Scotland in the second half. The first was that Wales fell into the classic trap of being unable to decide whether to sit on their one-goal lead or go out for the second goal that would clinch matters. Their attacks were curiously half-hearted and Rush contrived to miskick when a fortunate deflection left him unmarked and six yards from goal. Thomas was played out, so too James, and still the Welsh did not substitute while they were in a position of strength.

But the Scots could not score, and as time dribbled away, Stein looked ashen each time the television cameras cut to the bench. He could not delay a moment longer. The call went out to Strachan to come off while Cooper was the man told to get out of his track suit. It was a very brave substitution for Strachan was combative and skilful, with the confidence to hold the ball. In most people's eyes Nicol would have been the man likely to leave the field. Stein thought otherwise, sent Cooper on, gave instructions to throw the ball out left for him while Nicol intruded down the right. At once the Welsh defence looked acutely uneasy. Cooper filleted their right flank and squared the ball across a gaping goal. No one up, no touch. There was a plausible penalty claim when David Speedie went tumbling in the box but the Dutch referee, J. N. Keizer, was not to be persuaded.

There were only nine minutes of play remaining when Speedie drove a ball against the arm of Phillips and the referee indicated a penalty award. The Welsh protested furiously but although Phillips was hard up against Speedie, there is no doubt that an advantage had accrued to the defence. There could be only one taker of the kick — the recently introduced Cooper. Confronted with the best goalkeeper in the British Isles he slid the ball wide of him as calmly as if he were in a training session. The Welsh spirit was crushed. They offered no threat in the remaining minutes.

Amid the dancing and jubilation when the penalty went in, Jock Stein had remained on the bench. A photographer, anxious to capture his reaction when the final whistle went, came intrusively close and refused to move. Stein physically moved him, leaving the bench to do so. At the time, most television viewers must have thought that the incident involved an overexuberant fan.

Attention wandered back to the field for the last few minutes. Suddenly, the cameras swung again to the track side and Stein was being carried up the tunnel on the shoulders of some policemen. One's initial reaction was to think of it as a very sporting gesture by the police, then came the chilling double realisation that the police do not carry anyone off in triumph and that in any event the match was still seconds away from completion. Whatever had happened was very serious.

The game ended and as the Scottish side, victorious on the strength of the 1-1 draw, moved towards the tunnel the taut figure of Alex Ferguson barred them. Grim-faced, he told the players that Stein had collapsed but that they were to go back out and do a lap of honour for the delirious Scottish support. Meanwhile, there was furious activity in the warren of narrow passages leading to the Ninian Park dressing-rooms. The Cardiff City ground looks what it is, the home of a struggling club in a country where the sport itself has struggled more often than not.

An ambulance, urgently summoned, eventually succeeded in threading its way through the skailing crowd, hampered inevitably by the Scottish fans who wished to see something of their heroes in their moment of success. Resuscitation equipment was quickly borne into the room. Rumour and counter-rumour abounded. People gave each other instinctive and facile reassurances. He had been ill before. He had been hurt before. Always he had recovered, taken his place as of right at the head of affairs.

But not this time. It became very apparent from the grief-twisted faces of Graeme Souness and SFA Secretary Ernie Walker, from the look of knowledge that not even his years of experience could keep from ITV commentator Martin Tyler's eyes, that the manager was gone. The eventual announcement of the death was in a sense unnecessary for those watching.

A family friend, Tony McGuinness, was given the burden of informing Mrs Stein who had, mercifully, not been watching. Attempts were made at once to contact his son George in Switzerland. Later the Scottish team medical officer, Dr Stuart Hillis, disclosed that the first test he had done on the manager had shown no cardiac function. For the next half-hour the medical team applied emergency treatment calling on every last resource of techniques and skill. There was no response and at that point the procedure was terminated.

Dr. Hillis stated: "He probably began to feel ill midway through the second half. There was no reason to think before the game that there was anything brewing. It was a sudden death which could have happened at any time." There were those who claimed after the match that they had thought Stein to be looking unwell before play started but claims like these are commonplace in such circumstances.

Dr Hillis revealed that he had been treating Mr Stein for "an unrelated complaint" over the past year. There had certainly been speculation when, the previous May, the national manager had not been among those attending the funeral of the Celtic chairman Desmond White. Perhaps the real surprise was that he had endured as much as he had. One thought of the pleasant pressures — the Dunfermline Cup win of 1961, Lisbon, nine league flags in a row, five league cups in a row, the wins over Leeds United and Everton — marvellous moments, but pressure nonetheless. Then there were the days of black melancholic pressure — Buenos Aires and Montevideo, the failure in Milan, the numbing counting of the corpses in the Ibrox disaster. There was also a car crash which would have killed most other men.

As the news of the death spread in gently widening ripples, it was met with shocked incomprehension. What one had taken for artistic licence — the sailors of Nelson, the soldiers of Wolfe and Sir John Moore bereft and grieving in the moment of victory — was revealed as a true and basic human reaction. The Scots huddled together in drained, silent knots, automatically furling flags and removing the more garish signs of allegiance. The soon to be famous bunch of flowers appeared on the pavement with the accompanying lines, "Jock! Heroes live for ever."

In the middle of a thousand contending demands, Ernie Walker had in the forefront of his mind that a wife had lost her husband and two children their father. As soon as the plane carrying the team back had touched down at Edinburgh Airport, he was driving west to be with Mrs Jean Stein and her daughter Rae. All through that night silent buses and hushed trains were bringing the travellers back from Wales.

The funeral of a man so widely known and greatly esteemed had to be undertaken with care, although the formalities in bringing the body

9

back from Wales were thankfully few. Unless care were exercised, the funeral would become a media circus with vast uncontrollable crowds. The widow asked that the Scottish football public should pay tribute by regarding the funeral as a private family occasion.

A wish so expressed would never be disregarded. On Friday 13 September 1985 in glorious weather, more than 10,000 people lined the streets of King's Park and Croftfoot as the cortège passed on its way to the Linn Crematorium on the south side of Glasgow. The great and famous were at the service, the players from the first time round, Law, Henderson, the great Celtic side of the Lisbon years, the leading officials in the British game, the few close personal friends. There was a very real sense in which his friends were the silent, inclined anonymous men and women who stretched the length of the approach roads. They had seen Jock Stein as their friend and leader; where he was there was confidence and a feeling that even unlikely things could well be accomplished.

The funeral service was conducted by the Reverend Dr James Martin, High Carntyne Parish Church, a man with a lifelong connection with football. In the address which is quoted in full below he distinguished between the public Jock Stein and the private John.

Funeral service of John (Jock) Stein, CBE.
Linn Crematorium, Glasgow; 13 Sept. 1985
conducted by the Rev Dr James Martin,
High Carntyne Parish Church, Glasgow.

Short opening prayer
Introductory words as follows:

This is not the occasion — it is neither the right time or the right place — for declaiming a lengthy tribute to John Stein. Already a large number of tributes have been paid and there will be many more, all of them richly deserved. But we are gathered here in mourning to give thanks for him and to seek God's comfort and help in an experience of great sorrow and extreme need.

It is, of course, really two men we mourn today, two men in the one body. There is *Jock* Stein, football's genius without peer, known and acclaimed all over the world. Jock Stein, who has done so much for Scottish football and for the Scottish football public. Jock Stein will be grievously and sorrowfully missed.

John Stein will be even more grievously missed. John Stein — husband, father, grandfather, brother, uncle, nephew, cousin, friend and colleague. John Stein — warmhearted and generous, caring and compassionate, loving and beloved. John Stein, who has done so much down the years to enrich and enlarge the lives of so many who knew him. John Stein whom it was such a privilege to know.

Of the many moving tributes that have been paid to the man we mourn today, none moved me more, personally, than the one given by a Scottish fan interviewed on television in Cardiff just after the sad news became known last Tuesday night. He said, "It was a great result tonight but all of us here would rather Scotland were out of the World Cup and Mr Stein was still with us."

That fan was speaking for us all.

And yet, you know, in a real sense the man we mourn today is still with us. *Jock Stein* will still be with us as long as football survives. With us still, for example, in the performances on and off the field of the footballers who have come under his direction and his influence. With us still not least in the probable play-off matches and in the hoped for involvement in Mexico. These things will be an enduring memorial to Jock Stein, football immortal.

Even more important for us today, *John* Stein will still be with us also, very much with us, in the memories and in the lives of his friends and of his family, even in the life of the grandson he rejoiced to welcome but did not live to see.

This is a time both of sorrow and of joy, both of mourning and of thanksgiving. And it is a time for seeking God's comfort and strength.

We are going to sing together now of God's caring love in the 23rd Psalm.

Psalm 23: "The Lord's my shepherd"
  Scripture readings
  Prayers
Hymn 695: "Abide with me" (a favourite of John Stein's)
  Committal
  Benediction

Before we disperse, I wish to express sincere thanks on behalf of the family — and on behalf of Mrs. Stein, Ray and George especially — to all who have supported them by their sympathy in this sudden and tremendous loss. Your presence here today has greatly helped, as have your concern and sharing of sorrow. The family are most grateful to all of you and to all of those many thousands not present in this chapel today but who, they know, have the Stein family in their thoughts and prayers. Thank you, all of you, very much.

Eulogies, testimonials, tributes of all sorts poured in, some elegantly worded, others awkwardly phrased, still others almost maudlin but somehow the more touching even for that. The most extraordinary recognition of this highly unusual man was, in the eyes of most football men, that which was accorded to him on the afternoon of Saturday 14 September.

On a brilliantly sunny, warm afternoon, there was a minute's silence before kick-off in every football match throughout Scotland at all levels, in all places. It was an absolute silence, nowhere more so than at Kilbowie Park, Clydebank, where the home side were playing Rangers. The Ibrox support stood muted and thoughtful for the man who had for so many years outthought and outguessed their own beloved Rangers. They could have done him no greater honour, and in so doing they greatly honoured themselves.

11

THE PLAYER

Stein, as depicted in the souvenir pictorial album issued by Albion Rovers to celebrate the winning of promotion. The caption to the photograph describes him as John Stein.

1

BOYHOOD AND YOUTH

JOHN STEIN was born at ten minutes to six on the evening of 5 October 1922. He was the child of George Stein and Jane McKay Armstrong Stein and his birthplace was the family home, at 339 Glasgow Road in the Burnbank district of Hamilton. He was plain John Stein as his father was plain George and his lack of auxiliary names was to be typical of his blunt directness of manner.

He was the only son. There were three sisters of whom two died comparatively early and for these two reasons he was the focus of parental pride and hope.

He was a miner's child and Burnbank was most certainly a mining area. It was therefore appropriate that the leading newspaper story on the day of his birth should have concerned the coal industry. His Majesty King George V was visiting Edinburgh that day and Earl Haig was paying a call at the Royal Infirmary, Glasgow, but the chief item of news was the state of the mines. Since the deregulation of the mines in the summer of 1921 the coal industry had lost almost two million pounds. There was the beginning of a steep decline in miners' wages although in 1922 they were still 40-50% above the 1914 figure. Miners were pressing for the elimination of competition among the mine owners but their bargaining position was very weak.

Stein's upbringing was unexceptional and could be paralleled by thousands of boys in industrial Scotland. Primary school was followed by a spell at Greenfields in what was then called the Advanced Division. The education was traditional but basically sound. Throughout his adult life and especially while he was in the public eye, Stein's speech was invariably colloquial and he would make the grammatical errors which that colloquialism entailed, but he used words correctly and well and often achieved a simple, effective and dignified style in his spoken utterances.

His early environment was absolutely crucial in the formation of his character. Miners had gone from the short-lived boom which immediately followed the First World War to the bitter and protracted General Strike of 1926. From then on throughout the 1930s times were very straitened until the approach of war once again gave a last convulsive shudder to the dying Lanarkshire coal field.

15

It was taken for granted that he would leave school at 14 years of age after an education which was functional and without frills. Scots are fond of saying that their education system was and is the finest in the world without troubling to inspect rival offerings too closely, but although Stein never aspired to higher education he was well enough served by the system then in being. From schools such as Greenfield came not only miners but turners, fitters, and from the Glasgow equivalents, the men who built and fitted out the great Cunarders. Another interesting if indirect testimony to the Scottish schooling of the 1930s can be found in the popular press. Newspapers such as the *Daily Record*, the *Evening News* and the *Evening Times* made considerable demands on their mass readership who were expected to have a fairly extensive vocabulary and to understand allusions which were sometimes fairly obscure.

The teacher in charge of football at Greenfield School, Mr Gibson, remembered John Stein as a schoolboy who was primarily serviceable on account of his height, an extremely important consideration in schools football. He played a lot at school for there was a hole knocked in the wall which separated it from Russell Park, the dilapidated ground of the local junior club, Burnbank Athletic. Gibson made the point that Stein as a boy could be depended upon to carry out instructions. The picture given of the slow starter is remarkably consistent with his future career in higher grades of football. He was not particularly young when he became a signed junior player with Blantyre Victoria and he was in his very late twenties before he ever became a full-time professional footballer.

After leaving school Stein worked for a few months in a carpet factory but the job was not to his taste and before long he had exchanged the variable light of a Scottish winter for the inky darkness of the mines. He was shaped and moulded by his time as a collier. On the one hand, there was the genuine camaraderie and mutual assistance which was the hallmark of mining communities, on the other the over-fierce sense of loyalty which could under certain circumstances impose a deadening conformity.

The miner was the aristocrat of the industrial Scottish Lowlands and it is interesting to reflect that Stein belonged to the very last generation of boys who would go down the pits in the nature of things. The Lanarkshire coalfield was already all but exhausted and within the next ten years the work force would move to Fife, to England, to Wales, or leave the industry altogether. Hitler's war kept pits which would otherwise undoubtedly have closed in the late 1930s open for a few years longer.

Stein was often quoted as saying that he knew as a miner that he would never work with better men. What marked them for him was their co-operative approach to the work in hand, a co-operation which the cut-throat nature of professional football threw into ever sharper relief over the years ahead. He could never rid himself of the notion that professional football was not really a job, certainly not in the sense that coal mining was a job.

Pastimes and occupations were simple. Quoiting, wherein iron rings were flung at a mark, was a very popular sport among miners. All along the banks of the Clyde pitch and toss schools formed and re-formed along the lines of the permanent floating crap game in *Guys and Dolls*. Stein's life-long interest in betting may have stemmed from these gatherings. One of his colleagues with Albion Rovers, his first senior team, recalls him nipping out of a party to flip coins under a street light, a light which was so dim that it took some time to realise that he was simply flipping the coins in the air rather than tossing them.

On the other side of Hamilton lay the Upper Ward of Lanarkshire and another world. Here were miles of good farmland and some of the most beautiful scenery in Scotland with small market towns and rivers full of fish. Stein's Lanarkshire was vastly different. His was the county of mining villages and small unlovely towns, of whole districts whose sole function was to service the heavy industries of Scotland.

Football monopolised the leisure hours of the workers in the heavy industries. It is not just mere coincidence that the three greatest post-war managers in British Football — Jock Stein, Matt Busby and Bill Shankly — were born within 20 miles of each other, Stein in Burnbank, Busby near Bellshill and Shankly in Glenbuck up on the Lanarkshire-Ayrshire border. Throughout the inter-war period there was scarcely an English club which did not have a constant influx of Scots players from the three great coal-mining areas of Scotland — Ayrshire, Fife and Lanarkshire. In the latter county every village had its junior football club whose gritty ash pitch was enclosed by ruinous corrugated iron fencing while in a corner a small hut did duty as a pavilion. Burnbank, New Stevenston, Holytown, Cleland, Newarthill, Baillieston, Blantyre, all had at least one football team and often two.

Stein would have played football anyway, even if George, his father, had not been involved with Blantyre Victoria as a committee man. The boy was a beanpole, tall but skinny with a lot of filling-out to do. His build dictated that he would be a defender, so too his comparative lack of pace. He had played amateur and juvenile football with McDonald's Barrows Amateurs and in the early 1940s he was invited to play with Blantyre Victoria, having turned out before this with Burnbank Athletic in the Lanark and Lothians league.

By 1942 professional football was only being kept going with great difficulty. The government was aware of its value as a morale-booster to the civilian population but the call-up was beginning to bite and teams were experiencing trouble in fielding sides of acceptable quality. The fact that Stein as a miner would not be liable to call-up was a powerful additional incentive for a club on the look-out for new players and in 1942, in the autumn, he was approached by Albion Rovers with a request that he play a trial for them.

His first outing was against of all clubs, Celtic, and although the lanky novice floundered in the early stages, saw the opposition take a 3-0 lead and must have wondered whether he had made a grave error in accepting the trial invitation, he adjusted to the pace of the game and played a full part in a recovery which earned a highly creditable 4-4 draw. The next two outings were markedly less successful with Rovers losing 4-1 to Hibernian and 7-2 to Falkirk. Stein had now been the keystone of a defence which had conceded 15 goals in three games and he may have been more than a little surprised to receive a signing offer from the manager of Albion Rovers, W. Webber Lees. Most players in that position would have grabbed at it but it is indicative of Stein's self-belief at that very early stage that in his own words, "I hung off for a week or so, to see if a better offer came along". None did and on 3 December 1942 he threw in his lot with the Coatbridge side.

They had signed a player known as John Stein. In later years the story would grow up that he was Jock to his acquaintances and John to his family and friends but in his early years in football he was known as John and indeed is so described in an Albion Rovers brochure of 1948. It seems very probable that the change to Jock would take place when eventually he moved to Llanelly Town, a Welsh non-league club. That however was far in the future and, Jock or John, Albion Rovers now held the registration of the young miner Stein.

2

THE WILD ROVER

IN signing for Albion Rovers, Jock Stein had become a senior footballer and, to that extent, a success but in going to Albion Rovers he had not allied himself to a powerful or famous club. Like many another Scottish side its name gives no exact sense of location but home for Albion Rovers is Coatbridge, a town some 12 miles east of Glasgow which is entirely a creation of the industrial revolution and a testament to the nineteenth century's insatiable appetite for coal and iron in the industrial West of Scotland. It is indicative that the *Automobile Association's Illustrated Road Book of Scotland* devotes 15 lines to the attractions of Cockburnspath, a Berwickshire village of just over 600 inhabitants while the charms of Coatbridge, a town of which the population exceeds 50,000, require but two.

Albion Rovers were a rugged team from a rugged town. They had started in the Whifflet district of the town and in their heyday, just after World War One, they had moved to their present ground at Cliftonhill on the road up to Airdrie. The terracing was quite extensive but the tiny stand perched precariously on an embankment above the main Glasgow road. The great year of the club's history had been 1920 when Rovers reached the Scottish Cup Final and lost only narrowly to Kilmarnock. Gradually they became overtaxed in the top division, were relegated and spent the early years of the 1930s in the Second Division.

Coatbridge was savagely struck not only by the general economic depression which afflicted the West of Scotland but also by the decision to re-locate the major industrialists, Stewart and Lloyd's, in Corby in Northamptonshire so that even today there are many Coatbridge families who have relations in that town.

Albion Rovers would always struggle to be viable. The club was too near Glasgow and only the fact that those who were fortunate enough to be in work had to turn out at their jobs of a Saturday morning saved them. Many of those who would have been more at home spiritually at Parkhead or Ibrox contented themselves with a visit to the local ground during the dark days and early kick-offs of winter.

But for the war it is very probable that Albion Rovers would have regressed to the Second Division, but the dramatic events of the

An Albion Rovers side of the mid-1940s which defeated Airdrie in a New Years Day game. Stein is third from the left in the back row and the famous Rovers right wing of McIlhatton and Kierman are first and second from the left in the front row.

The dapper and youthful Stein with two of his Albion Rovers team mates before a match against Dundee at Dens Park in 1946.

summer of 1940 saw the Scottish League disband for the duration of hostilities. In its place came a competition called the Southern League and Rovers were invited to join. On acceptance they were free to play against the 'Old Firm', Rangers and Celtic, and the two major Edinburgh clubs among others. The major north-eastern clubs, Aberdeen and Dundee, were excluded on the grounds of geography.

The set-up had certain advantages for the Coatbridge team. There was no promotion or relegation so much of the stress of peace-time football was removed. Since the maximum permissible wage for playing football was £2 per match, and full-time football was prohibited, there was little chance of players being enticed away. Again, located as the club was in an area of heavy industry, many of the players were miners or in reserved occupations and there could be some continuity of selection. Having said all that, Rovers were perpetually straining against the collar and in the five years from 1941-45 they were either bottom or second bottom of the Southern League, contriving to lose more than 90 goals each season in what was only a 30-match programme. The defence could fairly be described as porous.

Conditions in wartime football were dismal and difficult. They are worth stressing, because Stein played longer with Albion Rovers than anywhere else and because they formed part of a dour, hard upbringing. To begin with, the players often came to a match straight from a shift in the pit or the forge, as their forebears had done in the game's earliest days. Full training could only be done in the spring and early autumn, for the rest of the year the black-out made outdoor work impossible. Food was short even for those in heavy manual work and clothing coupons had to be acquired for the purpose of obtaining strips. The first memory I have of Stein is in a faded blue jersey which looked slightly tight in a side which was being run ragged by a very powerful Queen's Park team at Hampden. For all that, the club had some smart players, if not well-dressed ones. The right wing of Johnny McIlhatton and Tommy Kiernan was particularly skilful and both players made it to the First Division in England, McIlhatton with Everton and Kiernan with Stoke City. The latter was in a sense to foreshadow Stein by returning from the south to Celtic although he was singularly less successful than his team-mate would afterwards be.

The press, anxious to engender what was often spurious competition in those wartime seasons would make obligatory references to the 'Wee Rovers', to their fighting spirit of 1920 and to the difficulty involved in winning at Cliftonhill. Most teams won there easily enough. Defeat was the Rovers' constant portion but it taught Stein two things. One was the importance of doing one's best in constant adversity, the other lesson was that the unsuccessful in football were not to be despised. He remembered and made a point of publicly recognising men who might have been thought by the sophisticated football world to have been of little account.

This, then, was the situation which the lanky young centre-half inherited. For much of the war he exchanged the blackness of the pit for the feeble lights of the war buses which took him back from matches and training. He looked a good catch for Webber Lees, dependable, durable, workaday — in the wartime sense of the word, "Utility", and he served them well for almost eight years.

One of his team-mates was Bobby Kerr, who joined Rovers in 1944 from Burnbank Athletic and was Stein's colleague for over five years. His memories of those days are very clear: "He was a great man for giving you nicknames. I was Breenger, because I breenged into tackles. He talked football all the time. He could never pass up a game if there was one being played anywhere in the neighbourhood. If Coatbridge St Patrick's (the local junior side) were playing he'd say, 'C'mon down Breenger and we'll have a look'. Sometimes after training it was a nuisance for I'd just discovered dancing!"

Kerr remembers him as a natural dressing-room leader, the man who would automatically take the players' complaints to the then manager, Webber Lees. Stein could sometimes manage to do a spot of personal

:NING TELEGRAPH, MONDAY, JANUARY 14, 1946.

THIS was Dundee's first goal against Albion Rovers, from a corner kick. The flight of the ball beat M'Innes, Gallacher and Stein and landed on the head of Juliussen, who nodded into the net.

A rare action shot of Stein in an Albion Rovers jersey. One wonders if the ball got Stein's length. Rovers incidentally appear to have borrowed a change strip from Dundee United.

negotiation. A dutiful rather than a devoted trainer, he was not above trotting off to the tiny office after a couple of laps of the track to announce to Webber Lees that he might have difficulty in making himself available for the next game as they were hard on absenteeism at the pit and he'd lose a shift. This sometimes meant that he was able to extract loss of earnings from Rovers in addition to the wartime £2 per match.

If he did not make the error of selling himself short he was normally very good value for money. Bobby Kerr remembers that a feature of his game was that he was at his best against top-ranking opposition. In those less tactically aware days, a centre-half was judged by the success he had in holding his immediate opponent and Stein proved himself master of such as Willie McIntosh and Jimmy Smith of Rangers, Arthur Milne of Hibernian, Alex Linwood of St Mirren and the other top centres of the day.

In Bobby Kerr's phrase he was "all down the left side and no greyhound" but he read the game well and would note possible or real weaknesses in the opposition. Even at this early stage in his career he had the trick of establishing domination over his companions. Thus, a worried team-mate, unsure whether he would get a re-signing offer from the Coatbridge club was admonished by Stein, "Aye, Tommy, you'll get 'flu lying behind the letter box waiting for that envelope to drop through".

To mark the achievement of winning promotion from the Second Division in 1948 Albion Rovers issued a souvenir pictorial album and in it Stein is described as "the best capture the club ever made. Strong, fearless, dependable, John (sic) gives little rope to opposing centre-forwards and his all-round ability and enthusiasm acts as a tonic to his mates. He acts as captain of the side — an honour richly deserved."

It may have been richly deserved but it was scarcely richly rewarded. Even in that solitary First Division season the wages were £5 per week when playing in the first team, with bonuses of £2 for a win and £1 for a draw. There were very few bonuses to be collected as Rovers, hopelessly outclassed in the First Division, staggered from disaster to disaster. Of 30 games they won three and drew two and they conceded 105 goals in the process. One of their rare and partial successes was a 3-3 home draw against Celtic but the latter were a very ordinary side indeed at that time and the result caused no tremendous surprise. It was believed, correctly, to owe more to Celtic's deficiencies than to Rovers' merits.

It began to look as if Stein was not fated to attract the attention of the mighty. Just up the road at Airdrie, Frank Brennan, a not dissimilar player, had been lured away by Newcastle United and gone on to wear a Scottish jersey with distinction. Nobody came for Stein.

With the inevitable relegation to Division Two his days at Cliftonhill were drawing to a close. He became increasingly dissatisfied with the financial arrangements especially as he was now a married man with a young child. Perhaps he was also something of a marked man because he had often acted as spokesman. The trainer, Jock Robertson, was not particularly a Stein man and preferred Sam English for the centre-half berth. The immediate post-war boom was receding and the increasing availability of supporters' club buses meant that the big battalions could be conveyed to Ibrox and Parkhead, undercutting the old local loyalties. It was time to up stakes but for the moment the job in the pits, although under threat, was still there.

He had eight seasons at Cliftonhill and had made 236 appearances, all but one of them at centre-half. He had scored goals, not many — nine to be exact — since he rarely came up for set-pieces and was not a noted penalty kick taker. With Celtic he was to be even less prolific, scoring but twice but, typically, those two goals earned three points. In the highly physical position of centre-half, he did well to be sent off only once, against Cowdenbeath on 1 September 1945.

The bigger clubs stayed away however and his last season with Rovers was unhappy, most of it spent in dispute over wages, a state of things which explains his restricted appearances. In the 14 matches which he did play there was one flash of humour when against Forfar Athletic on 3 September 1949 Stein advised his goalkeeper that a free-kick just outside the area was non-scoring. His interpretation of the laws of the game was unquestioned by his colleagues but they would have done well to question on this occasion. The free kick was dispatched to the net with the goalkeeper, Boyd, making no effort to save. The goal was immediately awarded. For once the big fellow was on the receiving end of the dressing-room barbs!

At last a firm offer did come, from Kilmarnock, who were still in the 'B' Division as the Second Division was called but who were a club with infinitely greater potential than Albion Rovers. Rather surprisingly, since there seemed no point in keeping a discontented player, the approach was turned down. The effect of this decision was twofold in the short term. Stein became increasingly desperate to get away and as his eventual destination was a non-league club, Rovers got nothing for him at the time of his leaving, for his destination was Llanelly, as the spelling then was. The change to the more Welsh orthography came later.

As ever in football transfers, there had been a linkman. Dougie Wallace was a South African of considerable ability who had come to Scotland to play for Clyde before the war and stayed on at the outbreak of hostilities. He had won a Scottish Cup medal with Clyde 1939 and was a proven goalscorer. He was good enough to be picked to play

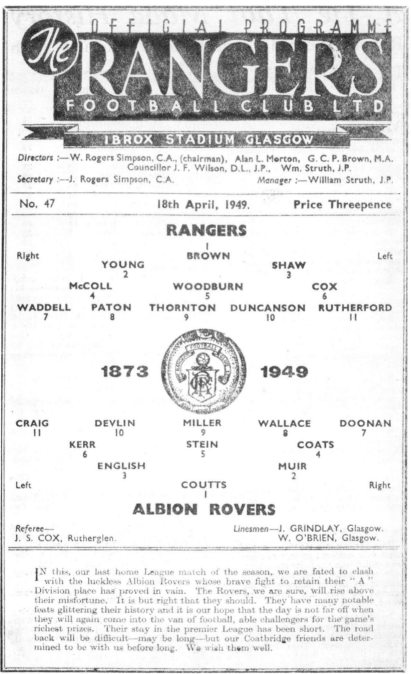

OFFICIAL PROGRAMME
The RANGERS
FOOTBALL CLUB LTD

IBROX STADIUM GLASGOW

Directors :—W. Rogers Simpson, C.A., (chairman), Alan L. Morton, G. C. P. Brown, M.A.
Councillor J. F. Wilson, D.L., J.P., Wm. Struth, J.P.
Secretary :—J. Rogers Simpson, C.A.   Manager :—William Struth, J.P.

No. 47   18th April, 1949.   Price Threepence

RANGERS

		1		
Right		BROWN		Left
	YOUNG		SHAW	
	2		3	
McCOLL		WOODBURN		COX
4		5		6
WADDELL	PATON	THORNTON	DUNCANSON	RUTHERFORD
7	8	9	10	11

1873   1949

CRAIG	DEVLIN	MILLER	WALLACE	DOONAN
11	10	9	8	7
	KERR	STEIN	COATS	
	6	5	4	
	ENGLISH		MUIR	
	3		2	
Left		COUTTS		Right
		1		

ALBION ROVERS

Referee—   Linesmen—J. GRINDLAY, Glasgow.
J. S. COX, Rutherglen.   W. O'BRIEN, Glasgow.

IN this, our last home League match of the season, we are fated to clash with the luckless Albion Rovers whose brave fight to retain their "A" Division place has proved in vain. The Rovers, we are sure, will rise above their misfortune. It is but right that they should. They have many notable feats glittering their history and it is our hope that the day is not far off when they will again come into the van of football, able challengers for the game's richest prizes. Their stay in the premier League has been short. The road back will be difficult—may be long—but our Coatbridge friends are determined to be with us before long. We wish them well.

One of Stein's few experiences of big-time football with Albion Rovers. The programme note at the foot of the page hints at a very unsuccessful season for Albion Rovers.

against England in a war-time international in 1943 but committed an appalling foul on the England centre-half, Stan Cullis, which effectively ended the South African's international career. He had spiralled downwards gently and had played a couple of seasons with Stein at Cliftonhill. His firm recommendation persuaded the Welsh club to send a man north and at the beginning of season 1950-51 Stein gave his signature to the non-league side. As an act of blind faith it equated with jumping off the Forth Bridge to find out if he could swim!

3

EXILE AND RECALL

WITH his move to Wales, Jock Stein became for the first time in his life a man whose living depended on professional football and this was to be his situation for the rest of his days. Significantly, his entry in *Who's Who* makes no reference to his time with Albion Rovers. This was certainly not snobbery on his part — no man was ever less swayed by such considerations — but simply his own feeling that until then his football did not mean very much. In his own words, used to Donny B. McLeod in a BBC television interview, "it was just a way of making money".

He would now make more money than he had done at Coatbridge. His basic wage would be £12, half as much again as he had got at Cliftonhill even when Albion Rovers had their brief excursion into the Scottish First Division. This was the heyday of non-league football in England with clubs such as Yeovil Town, Kettering Town and Colchester United drawing large crowds and causing several FA Cup upsets.

It was significant and saddening that a non-league club in England could offer better terms than a league side in Scotland which was then enjoying a period of comparative prosperity but the fact was that South Wales was in footballing terms an elephants' graveyard. Of the non-leaguers, Shrewsbury, Peterborough and Colchester would eventually achieve league status but there was no hope of that for such as Llanelly. The inter-war collapse of Aberdare Athletic and Merthyr Tydfil and the precarious existence of Newport County made it certain that any Football League ambitions which a Welsh non-league side might cherish would be severely discouraged.

Stein, as ever, gave his best endeavours but cut off from his wife and young daughter, it must have been a miserable enough existence. At a time when the West of Scotland was experiencing a savage and crippling shortage of housing, he had managed to obtain a council house in Hamilton and it was therefore imperative that wife and child stay behind in case the Welsh venture did not work out.

That fine writer, Jack Webster, in an article in the *Glasgow Herald* conveyed something of Stein's lifestyle and of his contribution to local football in those days in Wales: "Down in Mansel Street where Stein found digs, landlady Lizzie Williams showed me 'John's room' and said she treated him like a son. . . . Lizzie laughed at the time she told big Jock he could have a bath when she was out and that he would find the bath 'through there'. 'When I came back, he said, "Where the hell's your bath? I've hunted all over the house and out to the back garden, but I can't find a bath anywhere." ' Jock was then instructed on the old Welsh custom of the table bath, a short deep container kept under the kitchen table."

His keenness and evident tactical appreciation rekindled enthusiasm in the town which was more used to spending its Saturday afternoon watching the "Scarlets" at the famous rugby ground, the Straddy.

When Celtic, totally unexpectedly, decided at the end of 1951 that they needed short-term cover for the centre-half position and the reserve team trainer Jimmy Gribben dredged up Stein from the recesses of his mind Stein saw it as a miraculous escape route offered to him from an untenable situation. Back in Lanarkshire his wife was finding it difficult to cope on her own. The house had been broken into on two separate occasions yet if football collapsed and the pits again beckoned the council house would be an essential base.

The high pre-season hopes of this Albion Rovers team were not realised in the top division. Stein is third from left, back row.

When he signed for Celtic the public were spared the tedious "all my life I have wanted to play for Rangers/Celtic" quotation which is so much a part of almost all 'Old Firm' signings. They were spared it for two reasons. First, it simply was not true and secondly, and more important, Stein's signing was not regarded as sufficiently newsworthy for him to be quoted at all. Later he was to say with great effect that while he could not claim that Celtic were his first love they would certainly be his last, but at the time he would have played for anybody who came to take him away from South Wales. A few weeks earlier his name had been linked with Wolverhampton Wanderers before Celtic pounced and, curiously, 15 years later he might well have gone to Molyneux as manager if Celtic had not again moved for him. So desperate was he that on receiving news of the second break-in to his house he was making his way to Llanelly Town's ground to say that he would be returning to Scotland only to meet his manager hastening to tell him that Celtic had been in touch.

His signing for Celtic caused a certain amount of strained surprise, bordering on displeasure, in his extended family. There are few places in mainland Britain even today where religious tribalism flourishes as it does in Lanarkshire and attitudes were harder 40 years ago. With his background he had till then served the perfect apprenticeship for a Rangers centre-half and in fact only seven years later Rangers made a very similar short-term signing when they took the Larkhall-born Willie Telfer from St Mirren.

Stein who as a 23-year-old bridgegroom had married Jeannie Tonner McAuley, then 20 years old, at Gilmour Memorial Church Manse, Hamilton, on 3 October 1946 had in fact wed a girl from a Catholic family. In accordance with a well accepted working-class tradition she "turned" but in turning she was not so much embracing new doctrines as renouncing old ones — "lapsing" as her former co-religionists would have said. The marriage refutes the rumour that Stein's background was one of rabid Orangeism. There, even a marriage with a lapsed Catholic would have been regarded with extreme disfavour, given the baleful possibilities of lapsing back.

It was difficult for George Stein and other male relatives to take an unfeigned delight in any playing success that John might have with Celtic. George Stein had been connected for years with the junior club Blantyre Victoria. It certainly operated no overt sectarian ban and was indeed to produce Billy McNeill, Stein's captain and eventual successor, but the Vics played in Rangers strips and real success for them tended to equate with one of their players ending up at Ibrox every bit as much as winning the Scottish Junior Cup. This attitude was strengthened by the existence in the same village of Blantyre Celtic who naturally played in the green and white hoops of their senior counterparts and while equally non-sectarian in the strict sense, would have preferred their stars to shine at Parkhead.

For George Stein, therefore, paternal pride warred with natural inclination. His son was now a top-class footballer but certainly not with the club which he himself would have chosen. Henceforth, however, his son's workmates would be international footballers. That would have conferred kudos in almost any part of Scotland but in football-mad Lanarkshire the reflected glory was blindingly fierce.

Sign here! Stein, under the gaze of manager Jimmy McGrory, whom he would eventually suceed, becomes a Celtic player in December 1951.

4

IN A MAJOR LEAGUE

IT would have made an even better story had it been Robert Kelly
himself who dredged up Stein from his own memory and sent for him
as another boy David. In his latter years the Celtic chairman did nothing
to diminish this impression, to Stein's own quiet amusement. It was
however Jimmy Gribben, the old scout-cum-reserve trainer who
brought up the topic one day. He had watched him often with Albion
Rovers and remembered . . . something.

The move at the time meant much more to the player than to the club.
The supporters, if they had any feelings on the subject at all, saw it as
yet another instance of a supposedly major club being content to buy in
the bargain basement. He was fourth in succession for the centre-half
spot with Jimmy Mallan, John McGrory and Alec Boden all well ahead
of him. His role was definitely to be that of the rugged old pro who
might persuade young reserve players to obey basic drills and perhaps
acquire basic skills.

Sean Fallon remembers that his reception from the established
players was not over-cordial. Celtic Park in those days worked very much
on the system that the first team on training days used the home dressing
room and that there was a considerable gulf between them and the rest
of the staff. Such a restrained welcome was entirely logical. Newspapers
talk (or used to talk) glibly of "new chums" but in the professional game
any new signing is a direct threat to some player already on the staff. It
is expecting rather much of human nature that a man should enthuse
over someone whose avowed object must be to remove him from first-
team football.

The newcomer had a freakish stroke of fortune in his first week at
Parkhead when both Mallan and Boden went down with injuries. He
was pitched in against St Mirren in a home match on December 1951
and although far from match fit not only played well himself but from
the outset conveyed this strange ability to instil confidence in his team-
mates.

He held his place in the first team for a month, lost it again to Alec
Boden for roughly the same period and then came back in mid-February
1952. From then until he stopped playing four years later he was never

31

The new recruit. Stein takes the field in an early match for Celtic.

seriously challenged for the centre-half position. Sean Fallon, who probably worked longer and more closely with him than anyone else, remembers him as a player. "He was a good player, better than useful. He was good in the air. He didn't chase the game. He couldn't — he wasn't fast enough but he read the game very well. He was very good at disguising his one-footedness. He had to live down quite a bit of suspicion from the likes of Charlie Tully and John McPhail who didn't think he had done anything."

He was indeed good in the air and was one of the very few defenders in Scottish football in the 1950s who could hope to take on Willie Thornton of Rangers and emerge at least with honours even. Yet it was not his playing qualities which hinted at something exceptional. The Celtic side of the day, although comparatively unsuccessful, was nevertheless full of internationals. Evans, Collins and McPhail had represented Scotland, Tully and Fallon were Irish internationalists and the emerging Peacock shortly would be. In those circumstances how did the workaday Stein ever become club captain?

The answer is that he did because Sean Fallon did. Fallon was selected as captain for season 1952-53 and at that time the Celtic captain

Stein and his goalkeeper Bonnar appear to have a less than perfect understanding in this match against Falkirk at Brockville.

33

Battle of the Greens — Stein blocks a Hibernian attack in a match at Parkhead.

could nominate his vice-captain. Fallon agonised between his great friend Bertie Peacock and Stein before coming down in favour of the older man. The captain then broke an arm against Falkirk in late December and although he resumed his office in February he almost immediately damaged the same arm. This time Stein retained the captaincy even when Fallon eventually came back to the side. He was captain when, in winning the Coronation Cup in the summer of 1953, Celtic recorded their most notable post-war performance.

In absolute terms, Celtic were fortunate in having been invited to take part. They could scarcely be regarded as amongst the top six sides in Scotland at that time, let alone the top four. Box office potential rather than playing ability lay behind the issuing of the invitation. The club's penchant for the one-off tournament had not departed however and wins over Arsenal (1-0) and Manchester United (2-1) took them to the final where before 108,000 people they met Hibernian who were everyone's fancy to take the trophy.

John Bonnar, not perhaps over his whole career among the very top rank of Celtic goalkeepers, matched his game to the occasion and was superb as Hibernian counter-attacked fiercely after the loss of an early goal to a spectacular shot from the recently signed Neil Mochan. Bonnar, comparatively small, broke Hibernian hearts as one improbable save succeeded another. He kept Celtic ahead against all sense and logic until Jimmy Walsh secured a second and clinching goal. Once more Celtic had won a competition against major English opposition, repeating their feat of the Empire Exhibition Cup in 1938, and Stein climbed the Hampden staircase to receive the trophy. For the moment, Celtic were back on centre stage and they were to stay there for the next season, recording a League Championship and Scottish Cup double. The league win was especially meritorious given that at one time late in the season they were eight points behind Hearts. Stein in these matches was his quietly effective self. Comparatively seldom singled out in press reports, one had to read hard for the indirect praise, which was that opposing centre-forwards were seldom mentioned either.

He relished the publicity which came the way of a successful side. Harry Andrew of the Scottish *Sunday Express* recounts how he persisted in his efforts to become a national figure. "At that time we took a sports quiz around the country with people such as Charlie Faultless, the referee, and Jock Wemyss, the rugby referee. Jock [Stein] kept badgering me to be given a place on the panel but to be truthful we would have preferred a bigger-name player, someone such as Bobby Collins or Bobby Evans if we were thinking of a Celtic player. But Jock kept pestering us and eventually we gave him a chance. He was good too. He always had definite opinions on topics and was pretty fluent in expressing himself. And all the time he was making himself known to a lot of people."

Established player. John McPhail is the Celtic skipper in this team photograph from the early 1950s.

"Your ball or mine?" Bobby Evans appears to be asking the question of Steain at Shawfield. The Clyde player on Stein's right is Billy McPhail, brother of John, and later a Celtic centre-forward of great distinction.

In political terms, he was building a constituency. One of the rewards for the Celtic team which had brought off the double was to have very productive results in years to come. The whole Celtic first team went off to Switzerland to see the final stages of the World Cup of 1954. There Stein was able once more to watch his much-admired Hungarians, although an over-access of confidence caused them to lose the final to West Germany. He sat and squirmed as the Scots, after a comparatively respectable 1-0 defeat at the hands of Austria, were put to shame by Uruguay with a crushing 7-0 margin. The shambling nature of Scotland's team preparations — one goalkeeper only, several reluctant conscripts among the players, essentials such as salt tablets omitted — were burned on his memory, and no doubt prompted his resolve never to be faulted in matters of detail should he ever be given charge of a club.

If the decision to let his players learn from the best in the world showed the visionary Robert Kelly, there can be little doubt that his tendency to dictate team selection prevented Celtic from retaining the Scottish Cup in 1955. They had come within a minute or so of winning against Clyde on the Saturday when John Bonnar fatally misjudged a corner kick from the gangling, scholarly Archie Robertson and there

The winning habit — Stein as captain takes possession of the Glasgow Cup at Hampden.

Just in case — Stein stands by to give goalkeeper George Hunter a hand should he fail to cut out the cross. In this Scottish Cup-tie against Rangers at Ibrox in 1953 Celtic went down 2-0.

was need of a replay. Bobby Collins, one of the finest forwards of his day, was dropped for some disciplinary infraction, real or imagined, and Sean Fallon installed in his place. The latter was a fine defender and invariably expended his best efforts but was never more than a makeshift forward, although in fairness it has to be said that he had scored the winning goal against Aberdeen the year before. He could not find the magic touch again, Clyde took the replay 1-0 and Stein had taken another decision. Should he manage, he would not accept such changes with the same placidity as the more amiable Jimmy McGrory.

As it happened, there were to be no more playing honours for Stein. Early in the following season, in August 1955, he sustained a very severe ankle injury in a league cup match at Parkhead against Rangers which was lost 4-0. On the previous Saturday Celtic had won 4-1 at Ibrox. Weary, painful months of attempted rehabilitation brought the final realisation that top-class football was no longer a possibility. He made an isolated league appearance but wore the Celtic jersey for the last time against Coleraine in a close-season match in 1956.

He had run up against the dilemma that sooner or later confronts every professional footballer. He was facing retirement at 34 years of age. That was admittedly a full career in footballing terms but with the exception of the last three years he had made very little money from the game. War conditions and the perpetually modest circumstances of Albion Rovers had seen to that. His ankle precluded the possibility of

The Old Boss — Jimmy McGrory, inseparable from his pipe, in happy mood with the fine Celtic side of the early 1950s. Left to right: Jock Stein, Charlie Tully, Bobby Evans, Sean Fallon, Bobby Collins, Bertie Peacock and Neil Mochan.

Take it away — Captain Stein is home shoulder-high by his team mates after the Scottish Cup success of 1954.

The Celtic side of 1954 with the League Championship and Scottish Cup trophies.

the season or two in the Irish or Highland Leagues with which footballers on the way down often turned a penny.

Robert Kelly, however, wished to keep him in the game and offered him a job coaching the reserves. Whereas the first team, without him, slipped back to its old skilful, inefficient ways, people began almost at once to talk about the new attitude among the Parkhead reserves. The former club captain was prepared to spend hours coaching and talking. He could make things simple and comprehensible. Players knew, clearly, what was expected of them and he early demonstrated his quite extraordinary facility for putting his ideas across. Training at Celtic Park had in the past frequently been lax, still was at first-team level, but not in those sectors where Stein had taken charge. He would not tolerate anyone who had a talent and yet abused it.

The more perceptive players were quick to notice the difference in approach. Several years after he left Celtic Park, Pat Crerand recalled his playing days there in an interview for the *Celtic View* in March 1971: "There just wasn't the off-the-field direction in the Scottish game when I

Guests of honour — And not for the last time. Jock Stein seen with his wife Jean at the Celtic Supporters' Association rally in 1957. Such occasions would henceforth form a large part of his life.

The end of the line? — Not on this occasion but a later ankle injury was to terminate his playing career. Manager Jimmy McGrory at the rear is pensive but sufficiently re-assured to look away.

was a Celtic player. The players were well treated but as I said there was a lack of tactical planning. Jock Stein was working along those lines with the reserves and when he moved out the gap wasn't filled. In fact this was the main reason for my leaving Celtic Park."

Celtic in the late 1950s and early 1960s were fast, fit and often skilful but essentially they lacked direction. There was little wrong with the

The sweets of victory — With Mrs Stein after receiving the Scottish Cup following the victory over Aberdeen in 1954.

43

calibre of player signed, for as far back as season 1959-60 four of the Lisbon team were already on the club's books, the four in question being McNeill, Clark, Chalmers and Auld. It was however increasingly clear that the paternal benevolence of Jimmy McGrory was not going to bring more than the most occasional success.

Stein knew this and knew that his own methods could work. He also knew that he would not be given the chance to try them out at first-team level at Parkhead, not for the time being at least. He would have to put his ideas into practice elsewhere. But where? In the immediate post-war era there was very little evidence of Celtic players going on to manage. Normally clubs in need of a manager looked no further than the latest distinguished Rangers player to have given up the game.

There was the chance that he might have taken over at Firhill when the manager of Partick Thistle, Davie Meiklejohn, died suddenly. According to some sources an offer was actually made but Willie Thornton eventually came down from Dundee to take over. To become a manager Stein was going to have to move from the West of Scotland for the second time in his football career.

THE MANAGER

5

THE MANAGING OF MEN — DUNFERMLINE

THOSE who take an historical interest in football, who love the broad canvas of the game, tend to like the master plan, the pre-ordained development of the sport along certain lines and the sense of an inescapable destiny for certain individuals. The greater the contribution made to the game by a particular person, the more this is felt. There is therefore a wish to believe that when Jock Stein parted company with Celtic he was merely being sent into exile to gain the necessary experience that would bring him triumphantly back within a few short years. As with his earlier return to Parkhead as a player, Robert Kelly was inclined to promote this view of things.

It is interesting to observe that Jock Stein himself did not subscribe to this notion. In an article in the *Celtic View* of July 1970 he states that he left Celtic Park to find if he could make a go of managing players. "It might have been in the minds of the directors that if I made the grade I should be asked back but if this was the case I knew nothing about it." In an interview on BBC television with Donny B. MacLeod a little later he mentioned that perhaps Bob Kelly had thought that he had gone as far as he could go at Parkhead but that he himself was egotistical enough (his very words) to think that he could succeed as a manager.

Certainly he had always been keen to manage and as he came to what in any event would have been the close of his playing career he made a point of asking journalists whom he considered to be influential to put in a word with clubs that he would be interested in managing. One of those journalists, Jim Rodger, then with the *Daily Express*, claims to have been instrumental in obtaining an invitation for him to apply for the vacant job with Dunfermline Athletic, to be one of a short list of two.

It is fascinating if ultimately profitless to speculate on the subsequent history of Dunfermline Athletic had the directors appointed the other candidate, Danny McLennan, who was a useful player with Falkirk and East Fife and who would go on to coach national squads successfully in the Middle East. Stein himself thought that he had blown the interview when he responded fierily to a question which he assumed had been asked for the purpose of ascertaining his religious convictions. He went off for a meal in the local Carousel Restaurant with no expectations at all and was surprised to be recalled and offered the job.

MR. STEIN

If it seemed strange that someone with no previous managerial experience was to be given charge of a First Division club straight away, the answer probably is that no one expected Dunfermline Athletic to be in that exalted category within the next couple of months. Their league position was very grave. They had six games to play and required to win them all to be assured of safety. Nothing in their previous record indicated that this was remotely possible. They were not an untalented side and had some good forwards but the defence leaked like a colandar. The ground was run-down, depressing, with a long shallow wooden stand full of pillars which impeded the view of the playing field. From time to time Dunfermline Athletic made brave forays which ended with promotion but the club's natural habitat was the Second Division and they looked like returning there very quickly.

Stein, taking over on 14 March 1960, identified three priorities, two of them immediate. He had to win the very first league game after he took charge which would be against his old club Celtic at East End Park. He had to do something about the defence on the well-tried principle that there is no point in having an umbrella if your boots let in water. In the longer term he had to give the players a good conceit of themselves. Before he did any of that he had to forge a relationship of trust with the supporters.

He had the great advantage that most of them expected Dunfermline to go down anyway. He himself in his first public utterance if anything exaggerated the gravity of the situation which he had inherited. "The team is in a precarious situation. I have no magic wand but will do everything in my power to save them from relegation."

It is quite safe to say that no new manager ever had a more dramatic start to his career. Within ten seconds of the start of his first match in charge, Dunfermline were a goal up against Celtic and they survived various alarms and excursions to win by 3-2. The remaining five fixtures with one exception were almost those which a manager in Stein's position would have picked had he been given a free hand. Dunfermline were left with matches against St Mirren, Kilmarnock and Airdrie (at home) and Clyde and Stirling Albion (away).

The danger was the game against Kilmarnock, at that time second only to Rangers in consistency in league matches. A combination of good fortune and swift thinking turned things Stein's way. The game was postponed from the Saturday because Kilmarnock were involved in a Scottish Cup semi-final. Stein bulldozed his directors into going for a Monday match on the grounds that Kilmarnock would have their minds on the Cup Final if they beat Clyde (which they did) or would be down because they had gone out at the penultimate stage of the competition. Monday night it was and against the odds Dunfermline won.

They won their last four matches as well and avoided relegation

The young manager — In his formal dress Stein could almost be a manager from the 1920s. Following his arrival at Dunfermline however, he would be seen much more in a track-suit and his methods would revolutionise Scottish football.

reasonably comfortably at the end. Perhaps the new man *had* a magic wand? He had beaten Celtic in his first game, and, more of a performance in 1960, inflicted on Kilmarnock their first league defeat in 21 games. His team had won six consecutive First Division matches and no Dunfermline side had ever done that before.

The close season seemed longer than usual for the supporters but the manager knew that he would need every minute of it. He was now well acquainted with the players whom he had inherited from the previous manager, Andy Dickson, and he knew that for all their willingness they would have to be reinforced. He had been promised by the club chairman, David Thomson, that money would be available if he wished to enter the transfer market and this he now proceeded to do. He bought the fast-raiding winger Tommy McDonald from Leicester City for £3000 and a little later took the Irish internationalist Willie Cunningham from the same club. In Cunningham he found an eventual club captain and these two players of experience and ability would buy him time while he set up an organisation which would bring forward young Fifers of skill in numbers.

The new manager had no intention of indulging in a yearly flirtation with relegation. He had to instil the habit of positive thinking in the players and, equally importantly, in the Board. Before he was finished the Dunfermline players would approach matches against Celtic, Rangers and Aberdeen with thoughts of outright victory whereas they had once dealt in terms of margin of defeat.

Although their form was variable Dunfermline were never in danger of relegation during the season 1960-61 and they did well enough to finish runners-up to Kilmarnock in their section of the League Cup. When, therefore, they started their Scottish Cup campaign at Berwick on 28 January 1961 it seemed as though the season would go down as quietly satisfactory. The Athletic won easily enough by 4-1 on a ground where bigger names would struggle in years to come and they hoped for a money-making second round tie.

They did not get it. They were drawn against Stranraer at Stair Park where the likeliehood was that they would go out to a stuffy Second Division side before a moderately sized crowd. Long distances and little money appeared to be the way of it but they disposed of Stranraer comfortably enough by 3-1 and were paired against an Aberdeen side which had reached the Scottish Cup Final only two years before. The team travelled up to Aberdeen the night before. They had done this also for the Stranraer match. The manager saw it as part of his plan to make the players believe that they were on the staff of a club with major ambitions. The wide expanse of Pittodrie presented as little challenge as the tight confines of Stair Park, Stranraer, and despite the loss of an early goal Dunfermline astonished the Scottish football world by running away with the game in returning an improbable 6-3 score-line.

Stein was now looking for an easy home tie and he got it against neighbouring Alloa from the Second Division. He got other things too — a five-figure crowd and an extremely impressive and no fuss performance from a Dunfermline side which won 4-0 and in so doing reached the semi-final of the Scottish Cup for the first time in their history.

In the process, Stein was learning something about management. He had to stop the players treating league matches as tedious fill-ins between the cup-ties. The best way to do this was to make the one unlooked-for change, to wrongfoot the players in order to unsettle them in a way which yet made sure that they would be giving of their best.

The very large travelling support that followed Dunfermline to Edinburgh for the semi-final against St Mirren at Tynecastle was visible and audible evidence of the confidence that Stein had injected into the club. The feeling began to surface that this year . . . absurd — the function of teams like Dunfermline Athletic was not to win cups. But this side was durable and even after losing their centre-forward, Charlie Dickson, through injury with only ten minutes of the second half gone, they were capable of hanging on for a goalless draw.

The replay on the following Wednesday was a dour, dreich affair which fittingly enough was decided by an own goal in favour of the Fife side. Dunfermline would play at Hampden and Celtic would be the opposition, the club with which the manager had won a Scottish Cup medal only seven years before.

Two league wins followed and then with the approach of the final players began to watch themselves, to shun injuries and shirk tackles. Stein was in a black mood as the team bus bore his players to Seamill Hydro on the Wednesday evening prior to the game. He had just seen Clyde destroy his side 6-0 and although it was an end-of-season league game of no import it was a poor preparation for the big match. A few days at the coast were followed by a return to Fife for the finishing touches. The team for the final was quite firmly fixed in Stein's mind. Then illness struck. Tommy McDonald who was certain to play went down on the very eve of the final with appendicitis. The experienced George Peebles moved to the right wing and Dan McLindon, something of a fringe player, found himself a surprise choice at inside-left.

The crowd, a noisy 113,328, expected that Celtic would win. Even many of those who had crossed the Forth feared that they would win. The following players would decide the outcome:

> *Celtic*: Haffey; McKay, Kennedy, Crerand, McNeill, Clark, Gallacher, Fernie, Hughes, Chalmers, Byrne.
> *Dunfermline Athletic*: Connachan; Fraser, Cunningham, Mailer, Williamson, Miller, Peebles, Smith, Dickson, McLindon, Melrose.

The match was an extraordinary repetition of the first semi-final against St Mirren. Dunfermline lost Williamson with an early injury and although he hirpled back bravely he had to leave the field for good with 12 minutes left to play. Ten men reorganised and kept Celtic at bay thanks to fine goalkeeping by Eddie Connachan and indifferent Celtic finishing. Nevertheless the departing crowd on that Saturday afternoon were confirmed in their impression that Celtic would be the eventual winners. It was a fact of life that against Rangers or Celtic in a Scottish Cup Final a provincial club got one chance and one chance only.

Stein did not subscribe to this piece of folk wisdom. He remembered perfectly well that in his own time at Parkhead Celtic had thrown away a Cup Final replay against Clyde in 1955. He suspected that the pressure would be heavily on Celtic who had won nothing for their multitudes in four years. He had noted that Dunfermline had not been in the least overawed in the first match. He felt he had been handed a bonus by the opposition when, Jim Kennedy also having gone down with appendicitis in one of the Scottish Cup Final's more bizarre coincidences, Celtic did not go to the experienced and crafty Bertie Peacock but brought in the comparatively utested Willie O'Neil. The ex-Parkhead captain heard this news with grim satisfaction. He left out McLindon, who had overtaxed himself on the Saturday, and Williamson of course was unfit. Into the side were pitched David Thomson at centre-forward and John Sweeney at left-half and the teams therefore were perceptibly changed from the first match:

> *Celtic*: Haffey; McKay, O'Neil, Crerand, McNeill, Clark, Gallacher, Fernie, Hughes, Chalmers, Byrne.
> *Dunfermline Athletic*: Connachan; Fraser, Cunningham, Mailer, Miller, Sweeney, Peebles, Smith, Thomson, Dickson, Melrose.

It was a dark lowering night and the rain sluiced down. Dunfermline from the whistle were more tentative than they had been four days before. The goal was under constant siege but Connachan's handling of the greasy ball was superb. Gradually the defence drew strength from his sureness but at half-time Dunfermline had contrived only one scoring chance and that owed everything to a touch of eccentricity by Frank Haffey, the Celtic goalkeeper, who decided to go walkabout 30 yards from the goal and had to scramble most desperately to get back.

The game had gone 67 minutes when Dunfermline took the lead in the face of unrelenting Celtic pressure. A break upfield and a fortunate deflection of a Peebles cross left Thomson on his own and his accurately placed header found the net. The cup however remained to be won and as Celtic roared in on the Dunfermline goal, Connachan guarded his net like a man possessed, one save from Crerand defying probability. One fumble would take the game to extra time and then the shrewd money had to be on Celtic. The fumble, when it came, was at the other end.

Charlie Dickson made a token chase of a long ball which was Frank Haffey's all the way but the big Celtic keeper, perhaps already looking to where he would throw the ball, dropped it under no pressure whatsoever and Dickson, almost embarrassed, ran the ball over the goal-line. Two minutes remained. The cup was won and two minutes later a burly man in a spotless white raincoat was making a dash from the dugout for his skipper and goalkeeper.

All the way back to Fife ribbons of people stood in the rain, most to applaud the triumph of Dunfermline, not a few to celebrate the downfall of Celtic. Over the Kincardine Bridge the route lay through Valleyfield and the small villages to Rosyth and Dunfermline itself. At the town boundary the local band took over and played the open-top bus through the rain to the City Chambers. The *Scotsport* cameras of Scottish Television recorded the scene as the band played *The Happy Wanderer* interminably. Nobody minded. In his first full season Stein had made history. He had not only won a major Scottish trophy but, far more important, he had earned the right to measure himself against the best in Europe and he required a ground which would be a fitting setting for such contests.

For the remainder of Stein's time in Fife. a feature of autumn and

An early signing — At Dunfermline Stein kept a close eye on the availability of Scots players who had gone to England. Here he welcomes former Raith Rovers player Jim Kerray, returning after a spell in the south with Huddersfield Town.

winter in Dunfermline would be the crowded streets on a Wednesday night as masses of supporters scurried along to queue beneath the harsh white lights of East End Park. Only Rangers and the two Edinburgh clubs had trodden this path before. Dunfermline were delighted but Stein was determined that European involvement should come to be seen as part of the pattern of a normal season. He had no wish to have a one-off involvement with Continental football and therefore the league position had to be continually worked at if European participation was to continue.

David Thomson was allowed to go to Leicester City for £8,000 — an undeniable risk for he was the scorer of what had effectively had been the cup-winning and has thereby earned much popularity. Stein felt he could get away with the transfer. For one thing the transfer fee, although a modest £8,000, was nevertheless a club record. For another, Thomson was not a long-established player and if a third reason were required, perhaps the Pars owed Leicester City a good turn as the club which had supplied both Tommy McDonald and Willie Cunningham.

The European baptism for Dunfermline Athletic in season 1961-62, was something less than total immersion, being against the amiable part-timers of St Patrick's Athletic, Dublin. The first leg was at East End Park and in winning 4-1 Dunfermline ensured that the return game in Dublin could be devoted to sightseeing. They demonstrated their efficiency by winning 4-0 in Ireland and were drawn against Vardar from Skopje in Yugoslavia. In this game the first stern European lesson was learned. With a lead of 5-0 from the first match in Scotland, the return in Yugoslavia seemed nothing more than a tedious formality. The manager tried to convince the players that work remained to be done but they were inclined to disbelieve him. They appreciated their error after a violent match which the Slavs won 2-0 and there were times when the final aggregate of 5-2 looked like being trimmed considerably.

This was a lesson learned. There was no such thing as an over-substantial lead from the home tie and Athletic would have to learn to cope with foreign interpretations of the rules, with the vagaries of foreign diet and with less than dependable air-line schedules. At this stage Stein had achieved his target for his first tilt at a European trophy but he was not about to tell his players that. They were keyed up in anticipation of the draw for the quarter-final and he was well content that they should be so. The ballot gave Dunfermline a tie close to the manager's heart, for the opposition were the Hungarian side Ujpest Dosza. Stein's thinking on the game and his standards of perfection had been affected more than anything else by the great Hungarian side of 1953-54. As a Celtic player he had been at Wembley to watch such players as Kocsis, Puskas, Hidgekuti and Sandor destroy England and score six goals against them in inflicting the first-ever defeat by a

Continental side on English soil. The fact that he was there was an instance that Robert Kelly might be a cross-grained visionary but a visionary he most certainly was. His former player was now to be given the chance to break a lance with the demi-gods.

If, that is, he was still at East End Park when they arrived. Other clubs had noticed that this young manager could win matches and competitions. He could buy and sell players. He could make training interesting and he could handle the press.

Hibernian were anxious to take him to Easter Road to replace Hugh Shaw who was about to retire. Perhaps not wishing to remove himself from Europe, perhaps unconvinced that Harry Swan would give him as free a hand at Easter Road as he had in his present berth, Stein after some delay made a statement in which he said that his immediate future lay with Dunfermline. The critical observer would have said that he might have dispelled uncertainty by making the same statement rather quicker but he would do the same again some 15 years later with the Scotland job, first to disclaim and then to pronounce interest. There was a bit of the newspaperman in him and he was never above giving a good story legs. It is true that he had signed a contract with Dunfermline shortly after the Cup Final in May 1961 but although managers' contracts were rather more weightily regarded then than now, there would still have been no keeping him had he decided to go. The club would have been compensated for his loss — that was all.

The performance in Budapest against Ujpest Dosza, although a defeat, was something that Dunfermline would rarely better in their ten years of intensive European competition. Cammy Fraser withdrew with 'flu on the morning of the match. Late call-offs were becoming a Dunfermline cup tradition and Jim Thomson had no time to be nervous before he found himself on the field. Within eight minutes the Scots were two goals ahead, the first from Smith after only 40 seconds and the second from McDonald in eight minutes. The calibre of the Hungarians is best assessed from the fact that with ten minutes remaining they led 4-2 until in the closing minutes Tommy McDonald struck again to give his side every chance in the return match in Scotland.

To go down 4-3 was in all but the literal sense a victory. Dunfermline were now firm favourites to take the second leg and the tie and they found 24,000 Fifers sufficiently confident of victory to come out to see them. With a top price of 15/- (75p) for stand seats the club was in profit from its European venture and if it could win through and draw a glamour club in the semi-finals, it would be handsomely in profit. As it happened, the second painful lesson of Continental football was about to be learned.

This was, quite simply, that Europeans had a greater aptitude for prolonged, intelligent defence and a lethal quality when they went on the quick break. One goal after 51 minutes was enough to put the tie beyond the reach of the Scottish club. Shrugging off the initial disappointment Stein was quick to praise the Hungarians, for whose football he would always retain an affection.

His second season, while bringing no major trophy, was in some ways more remarkable than the one before. His men had performed consistently and well, setting themselves new standards of achievement. There was a best-ever fourth in the First Division which meant Europe, and a narrow defeat from St Mirren in the quarter-finals of the Scottish Cup. Add to that two victories and a very near miss in Europe, mention that the stand which had defied the years was being dismantled almost as the last home game was being played, mention that negotiations were taking place for a full-scale training ground, and it is clear that the Dunfermline directors were entitled to preen themselves on the sagacity of their choice. The manager had done something else. With a couple of league games to go he had slipped in to the league side a 16-year-old called Alex Edwards.

Over a close season a towering new stand had arisen at East End Park, the club offices had been transformed, the floodlighting system improved and, in general, the ground had moved to the front of those in Scotland. Stein used to joke that the new building should have been called the Cammy Fraser stand since the transfer of that player to Aston Villa for £23,500 went a long way towards paying for it.

Again Stein knew that he was taking risks. A Scottish provincial side has always to contend with the often justified fears of its supporters that the club is open to every and any offer for their players that comes out of England. Nor is it confined only to provincial clubs — at the end of the day the departure to England in quick succession of three noted Celtic players would go far to disillusion the vast Celtic support and make even Stein's position untenable eventually. Yet he was confident that the departure of Fraser would be accepted by the supporters. He once told me, "You can always get away with transferring a defender", and in any event the team continued to win.

The very existence of Dunfermline's role in Europe in the next season, 1962-63, requires some explanation. They had qualified on merit but had been rejected initially by the Inter Cities Fair Cup competition committee. They owed their invitation to the fact that the Greek club Salonika, one of the original acceptances, eventually withdrew. Dunfermline inherited not only their place but their opponents, the English giants, Everton, with the knowledge that if they came through they would be matched with either Celtic or Valencia of Spain. Everton were quite enough to be going on with. They had spent the awesome amount of £250,000 on their side and had dredged talent from every corner of the British Isles. In their forward line were found

Billy Bingham, Alec Young and Roy Vernon, who were respectively an Irish, a Scots and a Welsh internationalist.

Dunfermline played it defensively at Goodison Park — dirtily, the English press said, towsily and robustly were the words the Scots chose. They lost by the only goal and even that was disputed by Willie Cunningham who claimed to have headed the ball against the bar. There were demonstrations against the Dunfermline coach as it left and indeed it had not been a pretty game to watch. Stein, not a believer in defensive play, was unwilling to evolve the controlled system favoured by the great Continental sides and therefore on those rare occasions when compelled to play defensively, his team tended to follow the "kick it out the ground" school. He had encouraged his players during the first match at Liverpool to do a little promoting of the notion that "if you think this is tough wait till we get you at Dunfermline" to the Everton players.

There was an unusual feature in the return game, which attracted 25,000 people. The same team was fielded two games running, a sure sign of the manager's satisfaction with the role playing at Liverpool. The Scots flew at Everton and in five minutes — another example of the virtue of the pre-match warm-up — George Miller had scored and the match was back at the start.

The English side were quite unable to create genuine scoring opportunities and young Herriott in the Fife goal was never under serious pressure. Extra time looked certain when with three minutes to go Cunningham found Melrose in the clear — highly suspiciously in the clear — and the little winger ran in on goal before shooting past West, whose token attempt to save suggested that he too shared the widely held opinion among neutrals that the Dunfermline player was offside. Certainly film of the incident tends to confirm that impression.

The Irish referee, S. Carswell of Belfast, awarded the goal and no more than the Moving Finger was he inclined to alter what he had written. Home town decision or not, it could not affect the magnitude of Dunfermline's achievement in defeating a leading Football League side over two matches. There were even occasions when they shared the back page lead stories with the 'Old Firm', although Stein rightly resented the fact that Willie Henderson recovering from a bunion ranked equal in the footballing scales of importance with a victory over Everton.

The end of the European season seemed to have been signalled in Valencia where the forwards never got going and Jim Herriott should have stopped at least two, possibly three, of the four goals which separated the teams. Twenty years ago newspapers could in all seriousness say that a crowd of 15,000 was disappointing or, to put it another way, only one-third of the population of the town of

Dunfermline had left their homes on a savagely cold night to watch a match which their team started four goals down against one of Europe's finest.

The memory of that evening remains vividly with the author more than 20 years later. From the television gantry slung below the enclosure roof, one strove to keep the voice in a normal register as the Spaniards slithered to the very edge of elimination. The ground was barely playable but Stein worked on the Portuguese referee and the Spanish officials whose distrust of the playing surface was matched by their reluctance to spend any more time in Scotland than they needed to.

Four goals down meant that Stein was in the ideal position for risk-taking. He brought in the 17-year-old Alex Edwards and Jackie Sinclair, not his senior by much. The venturesome approach was at once rewarded. The crowd had a game on their hands after 16 minutes by which time Peebles and Sinclair had each scored. Another minute and Sinclair had scored again and with more than two-thirds of the match to go Dunfermline were only a goal behind.

Then, swiftly, Valancia broke from defence and when Nunez squared the ball across goal the teetering Dunfermline defence could not turn on it. Guillot, running in, had no such problems and Valencia had their two-goal cushion. But on a skid pan of a pitch defences were always going to be in bother. In normal conditions the Spaniards would not have conceded the goals to McLean and Peebles which sent the sides in level on aggregate, 5-5, at the interval. For the last ten minutes, the author as commentator had been totally unable to hear a word he spoke.

The second half began in silence, not because nothing was happening but because the Spaniards scored again through a lucky deflection from the head of Jim McLean and surely now the fire and the fortune were alike exhausted. Peebles did not think so and his run and cross allowed Smith, lurching like every screen drunk, to stay on his feet just long enough to shoot into the net before veering off wildly behind the goal.

And now the oddest thing of all, for Dunfermline for the first time in the match abandoned all-out attack and seemed fearful of the sporadic Valencia raids. They had over half an hour of play to win the match but they lacked the final touch of conviction in this period.

No standing ovation was ever more genuine or more earned. The players were recalled and recalled again to the field but meanwhile in the dressing room the toss had been lost for choice of venue for the third game which was necessary at that time. Guessing correctly, the Spaniards elected to take the tie to Portugal, technically a neutral venue but heavily favouring Valencia, although the most fiendish winter on record had also something to do with choice of venue.

In Portugal before a handful of spectators and on a Lisbon ground lacking all atmosphere, Dunfermline went out by the only goal of the match. They lost very heavily on the financial side but could console themselves with the thought that directly arising from the circumstances of this tie a change in rule would ensure that any third game would be played on the ground of one or other of the opposing teams, the toss of the coin to decide.

The remainder of the season was a stampede to overtake the daunting pile-up of postponed fixtures. Edwards played for amateur Scotland the night before he was legally entitled to sign as a professional. Asked if this had not done a genuine amateur out of a cap against England Stein growled, "The boy's entitled by rule to be picked. He may never get a cap at senior level." This observation, although judged highly improbable and pessimistic at the time, proved all too accurate.

The Scottish Cup was lost because it is difficult to beat Aberdeen at Pittodrie at any time but when you lose your goalkeeper with a fractured thumb after ten minutes and a forward (McLindon) gets himself sent off on the hour, then the difficult becomes the impossible.

The Cup side, even two years later was breaking up. Recurring injury meant that Cunningham took the first steps on Stein's journey and became a coach to the club. Jackie Williamson was also invalided out and Tommy McDonald moved to the coast with Raith Rovers at Kirkcaldy. New players were coming in — the two Callaghans and John Lunn, whose life was to be so tragically curtailed.

There had been no pattern to the season. The two month-freeze up in January and February had seen to that. If one thing was certain it was that clubs in Europe who could not have found Dunfermline on an atlas three years before were now eager to avoid them on balloting days. One man had brought this about.

What was to prove Stein's last season at Dunfermline, 1963-64, started well after a poor showing in the League Cup. After seven league matches the Fifers had dropped only two points and were leading the league. The most important English clubs were delighted to be asked to engage them in testimonial matches and Newcastle United came north to play in just such a game for Willie Cunningham and Jackie Williamson. Former favourite sons such as Cammy Fraser from Aston Villa and Eddie Connachan, who now kept goal for Middlesbrough, came back for the occasion. Such reunions could not disguise however that there was a rapid turnover in personnel at East End Park. The bigger stages were beginning to exercise their pulling power.

In November 1963 Stein was invited by the *Daily Express* to accompany Willie Waddell, who was then managing Kilmarnock, to go to Milan and learn from the coaching methods of Helenio Herrera. Stein and Waddell were the most representative of the new thrusting breed of young managers who had supplanted the more sedate Bill Struths and Tommy Walkers. They were mounting the only serious challenge to the all-but-unquestioned dominance of Rangers. For the moment Celtic, under the lounge-suited Jimmy McGrory, could muster no such threat. Walter McCrae, then Kilmarnock trainer, accompanied the two men and he remembers the trip thus: "Stein was captivated by the great man, by his ruthlessness, by his authority, by the fact that he was kept waiting, we all were, by him for an hour on the first day. He liked the routines which Herrera had devised for training and their contrast with the deadly unimaginative training sessions in Scotland. Where he showed great originality was in adapting Herrera's techniques so that the end product was fluent aggressive football, which he was to demonstrate against the master himself at Lisbon in 1967."

There had been some confusion at the outset, as Walter McCrae recalls. McCrae had introduced himself as the trainer and the Spaniards present, seizing on the word *entrenador* had accorded him the deference due to the manager of the side. But real lessons were learned. Quite apart from the negative aspects of Italian football, which he so disliked, Stein knew that there was no chance of the Scottish players being prepared to submit to the quasi-monastic existence of their Italian counterparts, whereby they were taken away from home for days at a time before important matches.

The Italian jaunt looked like paying immediate returns when Dunfermline raced to the semi-finals of the Scottish Cup. It is true that they encountered no very taxing opposition but there was a grim professionalism about them as they swept aside Fraserburgh (7-0), East Stirling (6-1) and Ayr United (7-0). All pleasure in the last result was lost in the news which broke before the match that Stein had decided to move on. In part, this was because he felt that he could never keep Dunfermline thinking of themselves as a major club, and he felt even less able to do this when David Thomson stood down as chairman to let the honours go round. In Stein's book, at the highest professional level, letting the honours go round was not a consideration. If you were good at the job, and Thomson had been a very fine chairman, then you remained in office until someone came along who was demonstrably better.

It is no great criticism to say that there was an element of self-interest in the move. The nature of football management is such that it makes very good sense for managers to move while they are on an upswing. Stein had given Dunfermline four years of unremitting effort and very considerable success. It is entirely plausible to argue that had he been of even average selfishness he would have left Parkhead and Celtic far before he did.

Having said that, the timing of the announcement of his departure was rather strange. He was not moving until the end of the season,

The track-suited boss.

indeed his very destination was not at first disclosed, and the knowledge of his going was the worst of preparations for the coming semi-final with Rangers. The resultant air of unease and impermanence in the Dunfermline camp may well have enabled a quite unconvincing Rangers side to win 1-0 in a bruising, unpleasant match. That game lost, there was no reason for him to linger. It was revealed that Hibernian would be his new club and that in everyone's interests he would be allowed to go immediately. Willie Cunningham, very different in style and temperament, would be his successor.

When Jock Stein moved from Dunfermline he took trainer Jimmy Stevenson with him but he left a remarkable inheritance. The club he had taken over in 1960, of small achievement, of minimal ambition, would remain in the forefront of Scottish football for five years after his departure, a long time in football terms. In that period it would win the Scottish Cup again, throw away a very good chance of the League Championship in 1965 and reach the semi-final of a major European competition, the European Cup Winners' Cup of 1968-69. If all that could be accomplished at Dunfermline, there were surely greater horizons in Scotland's capital.

6

AN EDINBURGH INTERLUDE

THE task which awaited Stein in Edinburgh in April 1964 was vastly different from the one which had confronted him at Dunfermline four years earlier. Then he had to instil the habit of winning into a club which had never won anything. What he now had to do was to restore confidence to a club which had been great only ten short years before. With Rangers, Hibernian had contended for the major prizes and although the Scottish Cup proved beyond them, they had won three league championships in the five years between 1947 and 1952.

They had won them moreover by playing the fast-flowing attacking football which could be expected to commend itself to Stein: they had been very much the Cavaliers to Rangers' Roundheads. The then club chairman, Harry Swan, was opinionated and made enemies but he was also visionary and among the first to take his club into Europe, first at a friendly level and then in the sphere of competition. To Hibernian fell the distinction of being the first Scottish club to take part in the European Cup. Massive crowds came to watch the Hibernian forward line, the Famous Five, Smith, Johnstone, Reilly, Turnbull, Ormond. In 1950 the New Year's Day Derby match against Hearts drew 65,000 to Easter Road and there were two-thirds as many at least for a benefit match played for the great outside-right Gordon Smith against Manchester United in 1952. The pedigree and the public were there in a way that they had not been at Dunfermline.

Hibernian in 1964 could well have been likened to an aristocratic family which had fallen on hard times. The forward line had all grown old together — most commendably the Hibernian board had resisted all but one of the English offers to buy them — and in 1963 the club had narrowly avoided relegation. The vast crowds were dwindling fast and power in Edinburgh had passed firmly to Hearts who were a very potent force in Scottish football in the late 1950s and early 1960s.

Stein quickly decided that he was not short of quality players. In Pat Stanton, Pat Quinn and Willie Hamilton he had three men of remarkable ball skills. He did not need much more in the way of artistry and significantly his first signing was the rugged John McNamee from Celtic who could be counted upon to bring pith and vigour to the central defence.

Not much given to second thoughts, a pause for reflection prevented the new manager from making a considerable blunder. His first impulse on arrival was to let Willie Hamilton go and on 20 April he indicated that the club was prepared to receive offers for him. Hamilton, a marvellously gifted player had an infinite capacity for self-destruction. Picked to play for the Scottish League against the Italian League in Italy he turned up at the Glasgow rendezvous in the dead of winter without the merest approximation to an overcoat. On a tour of Canada, given the man of the match award, a silver salver, he solved the problem of fitting it into his holdall by bending it in two over his knee. Stein was inclined to think that he was bad news and therefore expendable. Curiously, he reached the same decision about Pat Quinn on purely footballing grounds and rescinded that also.

The luck which had surrounded him continued to favour his first days in Edinburgh. In the summer of 1964 the League was experimenting with a Summer Cup competition run in four sections, each of four teams. There were 18 teams in the First Division then but Celtic and Rangers declined to have anything to do with the new-style competition. With one point from the first two games Hibernian interest in the Summer Cup seemed over as it was patently obvious that Hearts were going to win the section. The Tynecastle side, however, were committed to a tour of the United States and had to withdraw when the competition moved to the knock-out stage. Stein's men managed to force a play-off for the vacant spot with Dunfermline Athletic and won it.

The two semi-finals against Kilmarnock were memorable for the part played by Willie Hamilton. It was largely his inventive forward play that restricted Kilmarnock to a 4-3 win in the first leg at Rugby Park and he was the presiding genius in the 3-0 return win at Easter Road. A crowd of 18,000 turned out for this match, proof that the success-starved Hibernian fans could respond to an occasion.

An outbreak of typhoid in Aberdeen postponed the final, also home and home, until the beginning of August when 16,000 saw Hibs go down 3-2 at Aberdeen. There were almost twice as many for the second match back in Edinburgh where, with Hibernian a goal behind and a few minutes left, Stein imaginatively switched winger Jim Scott and centre-forward Stan Vincent. The cast of the dice came off and Hibernian, by winning 2-1 in extra time, took matters to a third game. This had to wait for a month because of fixture congestion but Hibs in winning 3-1 demonstrated their superiority very clearly and had thus won their first honour in ten years.

It was a minor honour and it was won with the 'Old Firm' not in the field. Stein well knew that. He also knew that in another sense it was quite unimportant, the habit of winning was what counted.

He had come to two conclusions. He could not afford to let Willie

Welcome to Edinburgh — Jock Stein arriving at Easter Road in April 1964 to begin a very short but highly successful spell as manager of Hibernian.

Hamilton go and if he could not reform him, he would have to tolerate his oddities. Ronnie Simpson could be allowed to go, and on the day after the Summer Cup success he moved to Celtic for a derisory sum. There was no clairvoyance in the move. Contrary to later legend Stein did not send Simpson on ahead of him to Parkhead. Their relations at Easter Road were strained. Simpson was not even playing reserve football regularly and had begun to ease up in training. Stein thought this betokened laziness and matters were not improved. Certainly the following statement by Simpson to *Evening Times* pressman Shearer Borthwick on 15 August 1964 reads like an instrument of abdication: "It looks like the end of football for me. I'm not unhappy at the prospect of hanging up my boots for I've had a good run and my job as a representative for an oil company must come first." So Simpson went off. He would be reunited with Stein at no great distance in time but such was certainly not the intention.

The latter busied himself with the start of the new season which began well enough although there was a certain irritation that failure to qualify from their section of the League Cup might just have been because he had taught his former captain at Dunfermline, Willie Cunningham, a thing or two too many as the Fife side nosed through.

After a bad loss to Hearts at home in the first match of the league, the results started to come. Stein wanted to get the fans talking and drive the 'Old Firm' off the back pages of the newspapers. He therefore enthusiastically canvassed the idea of a match against the great European side Real Madrid, their name legendary in Scotland since their masterly destruction of Eintracht Frankfurt at Hampden in the European Cup Final of 1960. Chairman Willie Harrower did the negotiating and although it took almost £12,000 to bring the Spaniards over, the match was arranged for 7 October. It is fair to say that Stein had three objects in mind in this matter. Primarily he wanted to see what his young side could do against the masters of Madrid, making all allowances for the non-competitive nature of the game and for the fact that Real were slightly beyond their zenith. He wished also to test the commitment of the Edinburgh public and, indirectly, to find out how ambitious the Easter Road Board really were.

He watched the Spaniards in training with a gimlet eye and showed the fussiness about goalkeeping which was his trademark in an observation to young Willie Wilson, the Hibernian goalkeeper. "Did you see that winger turn that shot? You'll have to watch that. You can't wait and let it come to you."

If he was worried the *Scotsman* reporter was not. He regarded the match as a foregone conclusion — for Real Madrid. "Hibs are not in the same league but that's not to say they won't fight like demons to prevent goals and to try and score some themselves. . . . It is certain that Real

Madrid will not lose. There is too much prestige at stake for that."

Real lost 2-0 and the crowd turned out in droves, 32,000 of them, a great relief since there was an appalling lack of covered accommodation at the ground and crowds were therefore more than usually vulnerable to the weather. The *Scotsman* reporter ate his words manfully. "Hamilton, the man discarded by so many clubs, was worth six of Puskas."

Suddenly Hibernian were the most talked-about side in Scotland and they continued to dominate the sports pages when on the following Saturday they went to Ibrox and defeated Rangers 4-2 after twice having been behind. Immediately afterwards, and rather ominously, it was announced that Jim Scott was about to be transferred to Wolverhampton Wanderers. Stein put a gloss on it by saying that he had two other players of equivalent quality in Neil Martin and Stan Vincent but the latter was hard-working rather than particularly gifted. At the eleventh hour Wolves drew back from the transfer but uncertainty had been created among players and supporters, as the manager admitted. "The whole affair has given contented players the notion that the club is prepared to transfer players willy-nilly."

The Wolves bid for Scott is very revealing in that it illustrates perfectly the transformation wrought by Stein almost in a matter of weeks rather than months. Scott had been up for transfer for the whole of the previous season without attracting a single offer and now apparently Wolves had been prepared to bid £40,000 for him. The side took full points from their league matches in October and by the end of that month had won their last six away matches. League form was very consistent although there was another stumble against Dunfermline in late November. The manager made a substantial profit for his club when he transferred the Irish international full-back Parke to Sunderland for £30,000 (he had cost Hibernian exactly half of that just over a year before) which more than covered the price of Parke's replacement, Joe Davis from Third Lanark.

By New Year's Day 1965 Hibernian were looking very possible winners of the Scottish League. They had taken seven points from a possible eight in December and on 1 January a Willie Hamilton goal gave them victory over Hearts at Tynecastle, a result which sent the normally dour and undemonstrative Stein jumping high with delight. Even a defensive nightmare which saw four goals conceded at home to Dundee United was soothed by the completion of the league double over Rangers with more than 44,000 crammed on the Easter Road terracing. The supporters were jubilant — this would be their year.

And then their world fell about them. On 1 February, it was announced that Stein would be leaving Edinburgh and going back to assume the managership of Celtic. The move would take effect from the end of the season or earlier, depending on the arrival of a suitable replacement. It was the first though not the last time that Stein would leave a club after a very brief spell with them but in the case of Hibernian there seemed little or no animus towards him.

Chairman William Harrower spoke of the pleasantness of the parting, regrettable though it was, and stressed that there were no strained relations between the people concerned. He paid unstinting tribute to the man who in a very short time had turned Hibs around: "During his short time with us Mr Stein and I built up a strong friendship. We spoke the same language. We were not afraid to tell each other that one or the other was wrong. No offence was taken. All our differences were conducted on a friendly basis."

The move was not likely to help the players who were left behind at Easter Road and there was an immediate reaction when they could only manage a draw against East Stirling at home in the Scottish Cup but they recovered to win the replay with something in hand and before Stein said his last farewells they had further eliminated Partick Thistle and Rangers (their third victory of the season over the Ibrox side) from the same competition. The outgoing manager left his men the league and the cup as real possibilities and it is the measure of his loss that they were unable to take either.

The receiving club, Celtic were naturally jubilant and Robert Kelly quickly moved to the manifest destiny theory. "He left Celtic because like everyone else he had to learn his trade but there was always the understanding that he would return. I want to emphasise that this is not a panic change. We are doing this when the team is winning and when we think that we have got a good team."

The Celtic offer had in a sense come too soon for Stein ideally, but the Parkhead club had heard rumours that an English club, Wolverhampton Wanderers, were about to pounce for the young and highly successful manager. Stein was flattered, as who would not have been, to be offered the Celtic managership and he felt a sense of profound obligation to the club. By an odd coincidence his successor, Billy McNeill, would be given the offer of the Celtic job just as he had happily established himself with another club, Aberdeen.

At all events Stein understandably felt that the Celtic invitation, once rejected, would not readily be extended again. He turned his back on Edinburgh and in March 1965 became for the second time in his life a paid employee of the Celtic Football Club.

The last word on the impact which he had made on football in the East of Scotland can safely be left with the football correspondent of the *Scotsman* at that time, John Rafferty, who on the day of Stein's leaving struck his prophetic lyre to considerable effect: "With Jock Stein in charge at Celtic Park and with his influence being vigorously carried forward by Willie Cunningham and Bob Shankly in the east, no longer will Rangers find titles and cups so easy to win. From now on Rangers will be unable to claim that home competition is too soft. Their easy reign is over. Jock Stein will see to that and at the end of the day that will be one of the best things that ever happened in Scottish football."

7

CELTIC — UNDER NEW MANAGEMENT, MARCH 1965

STEIN'S transfer from Hibernian to Celtic was in the end rather untidy. The statement released by the Hibernian Board at the news conference of 31 January 1965 had said that he would go at the end of the season or earlier if Hibernian found a suitable replacement. In a bewildering all-change of Scottish managers Bob Shankly took over from Stein at Easter Road, his place at Dundee being taken by Bob Ancell of Motherwell, with Bobby Howitt succeeding to the vacant Fir Park chair. It was 10 March by the time Stein arrived at Parkhead and his first service to his new club had been to eliminate Rangers from the Scottish Cup on his last afternoon in charge of Hibernian.

In moving to Celtic Stein was gambling on potential rather than achievement as far as the club itself was concerned. On that day the majority of observers would have said that Hibernian, conquerors of Rangers and very probable league champions had more to offer a really ambitious manager. The Cup in particular seemed theirs for the taking. In the mid-1960s Rangers were the team to beat and any side which managed this was automatically installed as favourite for the competition. Much later Stein was to say that considering things purely from the point of view of playing strength he would have been just as happy taking over at Ibrox.

Celtic's record since the end of World War Two had been sadly undistinguished. The club could rise to the brilliant one-off performance such as the 7-1 destruction of Rangers in the 1957 League Cup Final. There had always been an ability to win the exotic tournaments of which the Empire Exhibition Tournament in 1938, the St Mungo Cup of 1951 and the Coronation Cup of 1953 may serve as examples.

Talented players abounded, Collins, Fernie, the McPhail brothers, Tully, Evans, Peacock, but consistent team performance was visibly lacking. The 20 years since 1945 had produced the miserable total of one League Championship, two Scottish Cups and two League Cups from 60 starts and for the great preponderance of that time Celtic simply could not be taken seriously as potential league champions. Power and ability remained with Rangers and any challenge to them was mounted by the two Edinburgh clubs, Dundee and Aberdeen. Out of habit the press continued to refer to the 'Old Firm' but this term had long ceased to denote a partnership or even a rivalry of equals. At Celtic Park young players came to the dilapidated ground and left without making any major impact on the game. The supporters, starved of success in the seven years from 1958, took refuge in complaining of injustices, real and imagined and increasingly stayed away.

On the surface therefore, Celtic did not appear all that promising a prospect and there were other complications. The retiring manager, Jimmy McGrory, was not only universally respected in football as a man, he was beloved by the Celtic support. Moreover, he was now to fill one of the two posts which would not be in the new man's gift. He was nominated by Robert Kelly to the new post of Public Relations Officer although from the beginning any really important announcements affecting the club were made by Robert Kelly or Jock Stein himself. It was potentially a tricky situation but in the event it never proved to be a problem thanks to the inherent qualities of the two men involved. There was not an envious bone in Jimmy McGrory's body and the new manager had a profound regard for the old.

The other staff position which had already been determined on Stein's arrival was that of coach, a post in which that excellent club servant, Sean Fallon, had been confirmed. It was not yet a totally accepted practice in football that a new manager brought his coach with him but Stein may have seen this as a certain limitation on his freedom of action.

There was another doubt. Robert Kelly had promised that he would be allowed to manage, but would he? Football has known no straighter man than the then Celtic chairman. His highly direct honesty could be almost uncomfortable at times and no one questioned his sincerity, but Jimmy McGrory had not managed in any active sense of the word and the chairman's word had been law. Old habits die hard.

The attractions of the job for Jock Stein were easily stated. The team had not been doing well so it should not be impossible to bring about a noticeable improvement in results. There was a vast following ready to be brought back, heart-sick of being humiliated, desperately seeking a leader that they could cheer. There had been some indication from the European Cup Winners' Cup of 1963-64 that there were players good enough for Europe. Lack of tactical awareness had allowed a 3-0 home victory over MTK Budapest to be overtaken in a 4-0 defeat in Hungary but the important thing was that MTK, a good European side, had been taken apart in Glasgow.

Crucially, Stein knew the young Celtic players and had been involved in the coaching of many of them. His immediate task was to bring the virtues accepted in Scotland as Presbyterian — industry, attention to detail, consistency of performance — to a club which had all too faithfully conformed to the stereotyped image of the Gael, volatile, variable, a touch feckless.

Jimmy Gribben. "He had seen Stein and remembered . . . something."

A man possessed of a keen sense of history, Stein must have been flattered by the notion of being the first non-Catholic manager of Celtic. The fact that the new man was at least nominally Presbyterian caused some excited comment in the popular press and references to Celtic's first non-Catholic manager abounded. The statistically minded chairman pointed out that the heading "One in four of Celtic managers are non-Catholics" would have been equally accurate as only three people had held the post before Stein in the club's 77-year existence to that point.

In popular mythology, Jock Stein arrived at Parkhead and overnight transformed the situation. This is largely true but it was not quite as immediate an improvement. In his very first game as manager of Celtic there was a resounding 6-0 win at Airdrie when the recently returned Bertie Auld scored five goals, but the next few weeks brought defeats from St Johnstone and Partick Thistle and heavy defeats at the hands of Hibernian and Falkirk.

The loss to Partick Thistle came on the Saturday before the Scottish Cup Final tie against Dunfermline Athletic, and Celtic had reached that stage by a none too convincing semi-final performance against Motherwell that required two matches to reach a decision. In the programme issued for the Thistle match Stein made a public and pointed attack on his new charges: "Consistency of performance must be the first priority. And several of the current players are not providing that. They have had their chance and they should know that I have been in England, looking."

The *Glasgow Herald's* scholarly reporter, Raymond Jacobs, thought this an injudicious pronouncement and said so. "It is surely not only untimely but unwise to run the risk of compromising future plans by so open and binding a statement of intent. This is a time, one would think, to keep one's own counsel." The castigation was certainly ineffective on that Saturday afternoon, for the last match before the Cup Final was lost and the crowd booed the team off the field. It would be a long time before that happened again at Parkhead for Stein had done much more than sound off about his players' shortcomings. He had made positional switches and changes in personnel that were to be very important. Always a quick analyst and almost always an accurate one, he had looked at that very first team he fielded against Airdrie, a team, it is worth remembering, which had won by a six-goal margin. That selection read: Fallon; Young, Gemmell, Clark, McNeill, Brogan, Chalmers, Murdoch, Hughes, Lennox, Auld. But within days it was altered substantially.

Stein thought that Hughes and Gemmell were not quite ready, although Hughes was comparatively experienced by then, and although he reintroduced Jimmy Johnstone quickly, he was discarded before the

Cup Final. His master switch was that of Bobby Murdoch to midfield. from inside-right to right-half in the traditional terms that were just beginning to fall into disuse. The decision on Murdoch had a wider significance. The chairman, Robert Kelly, queried the projected move and expressed doubts on the capacity of the player to adapt. "Watch on Saturday and you'll see if he's a half-back or not," said the new manager and the meaning was unmistakable. Henceforth he would take the on-field decisions.

Whenever it was suggested to Napoleon Bonaparte that a general be made a Marshal of France, the Emperor had one standard question, "Is he lucky?" It was a trait that he esteemed highly, the more so that he regarded luck as, in his own words, "the residuum of good planning". Stein was to meet Napoleon's requirements in the 1965 Scottish Cup Final when he quite cheerfully admitted that Celtic had been a shade lucky to defeat Dunfermline Athletic 3-2 at the first attempt. A very small swing of fortune would have sent the trophy back to Dunfermline where he himself had taken it four short years before.

Yet, lucky or not, Celtic had twice in the match fought back from a goal behind, had recorded their first major success in seven years and

Triumphant return — Stein greeted by enthusiastic fans following a successful European trip.

had shown a fierce commitment on the day. From the outset, Stein starkly discerned those matches that mattered to his overall strategy. Thus a 5-1 defeat by Dunfermline the very next week in a postponed league game was a bad result for Celtic and soothed Fife pride but it was far more important to hammer Queen's Park 5-0 in the Glasgow Charity Cup Final. It was not that he attached any great value to that competition, which in any event was on its last gasp, but Celtic had to be seen to have regained the habit of trophy-winning.

On 1 May 1965 Stein made his first radical change in the operation of the playing side. No fewer than 20 players were released. There were no big names, all of them were youngsters, and even then the playing staff was still a healthy 31-strong. Henceforth, there would be no third team and the coaching staff would concentrate its energies on the first eleven and the reserves. There would be two daily training sessions at the practice ground, Barrowfield, and an evening stint would accommodate the part-timers.

It was an eventful time at Parkhead. Four days later, on 5 May, Celtic announced that the club would publish a weekly magazine, the *Celtic View*. This was the highly original concept of Jack McGinn who was later to join the Board, and his notion was received by Jock Stein with the *panache* which was to become his trademark: "Have the first issue ready for the week after the Cup Final and leave a blank space on Page 1 for a picture of the boys with the cup." Dunfermline were, as we have seen, met and overcome but not the deadline and the first issue appeared in August 1965. This in no way diminished the manager's enthusiasm for the publication. It could, he thought, achieve several objectives for him. He saw the magazine as a way to instruct supporters in the history of the club, to acquaint them with current developments, or at least certain selected current developments, and, most usefully, to establish a code of behaviour for the guidance of the fans. In all this he was and remained a genuine populist.

Suddenly, the home season which he had started with Hibernian was over. In the course of it Hibernian had won the Summer Cup, beaten Real Madrid once and Rangers three times. With Celtic, there had been the Scottish Cup and Glasgow Charity Cup victories. Wider recognition of these successes was immediate. He was asked to look after the Scotland side for the forthcoming away matches against Poland and Finland in the World Cup, following the dismissal of the team manager Ian McColl. He agreed to act as caretaker, to provide, in the baseball phrase, short-term pitching relief.

He went to Europe leaving an unresolved problem at Parkhead. He needed a proven goal-scorer and thought of Joe McBride of Motherwell who had played Celtic virtually on his own in the first of the two semi-final meetings in the Scottish Cup. Stein persuaded the Board to make an offer but the initial bid of £20,000 was rejected. Dunfermline, that canny provincial club of limited resource, were said to have bid £25,000 for the player. The new manager would have to persuade his directors to think big, and persuade them quickly.

8

THE INTERNATIONAL MAN — FIRST TIME ROUND

IT was not at all surprising that when in the early summer of 1965 the Scottish selectors found that their views on national team policy differed from those of Mr Ian McColl, the former Rangers' wing-half, they should turn in the direction of Jock Stein as a temporary replacement. Given Scotland's extremely chequered career at this level it is slightly strange that Mr McColl was not perceived to be doing a reasonably efficient job. In the one World Cup qualifying match played to that date Scotland had defeated Finland 3-1 at Hampden Park and although confronted with a depleted England team at Wembley there had been worse Scottish results than a 2-2 draw.

Mr McColl, however, was not thought sufficiently authoritative and was so informed by the secretary of the SFA, Mr Willie Allan. Stein, in view of his record at Dunfermline and Easter Road and his auspicious start at Celtic Park, was the man to transmute base metal into gold. Since he had at his disposal players such as Jim Baxter, Denis Law, Willie Henderson, Charlie Cooke and Bobby Murdoch, the metal was not all that base, although there would clearly be problems of temperament and of attitude.

It would be a compressed World Cup campaign with the return match against Finland and the fixtures with the other two group members, Poland and Italy, all due in less than seven months. Initially Stein agreed to look after the squad for the away matches in Poland and Finland. The Polish venture could fairly be said to be successful. A 1-1 draw against one of the stronger European countries in a grimy, uninspiring factory town, Chorzow, was a good start. He had kept the squad happy in hostel-like accommodation and Denis Law had now scored in two consecutive World Cup matches.

Technically the position on team selection was that the manager could advise after the selectors had nominated the players in the squad. What was now needed was an emphatic win against Finland to boost goal average and confidence. Stein had his way over team choice. He dropped two players with Parkhead connections, John Hughes and Bobby Collins, and brought in two players whose boss he had been two short months before, Neil Martin and Willie Hamilton of Hibernian.

The idea was that Hughes was being left out in favour of a direct attacking policy. In Stein's words, "Teams must be chosen with a specific end in view". Nothing in his managerial career would be more astounding than his ability with Celtic to make the single profitable change week in, week out.

The team against Finland disappointed but won nevertheless, and three points had been guaranteed from a possible four. If the same return could be obtained from the forthcoming home matches against Poland and Italy, the last match of all, the return in Italy might be of very little significance. Stein's thinking was geared to ensuring that it would in fact be a dead match.

It was a happy Scottish party that flew home. The Press were delighted with the new manager. He had been as forthcoming and understanding of their problems as the previous manager, Ian McColl, had been introverted and withdrawn. The reporters may have established a precedent when they made a small in-flight presentation to both Stein and trainer Walter McCrae. The adverse conditions in Poland had been good for team spirit. Little things such as the players eating the food that McCrae had brought with them while for once the officials had to make do with the restricted Polish diet, helped to weld the Scots into a purposeful unit.

Stein had also taken the opportunity to show that he would enforce discipline where necessary. On the first evening's bed-check in Poland some half-dozen of the Scottish side were discovered playing cards well after lights out. Stein's entry to the room was followed by a few terse sentences, some impressive ripping of playing cards and their consignment to the lavatory bowl. The players took the hint and went to bed.

George Aitken in the *Evening Citizen* described him as "disciplinarian, diplomat, laughter-maker" and hinted that he was certain to be offered the job on a permanent basis, but Celtic did not favour this. There was a strong feeling among reporters that the Stein-McCrae partnership was potentially a winner. The latter had endeared himself to the manager by his capacity and willingness to work non-stop for long periods to ensure that the players were well fed and carefully treated. He had insisted on being allowed access to supervise the preparation of food in the somewhat grubby kitchen and submitted to wearing a white coat which was by far the cleanest object in sight. In years to come Walter McCrae would become a successful manager himself with Kilmarnock and was quick to acknowledge those areas where he had learned much from watching Stein at work.

From the outset Stein's approach was marked by a fanatical attention to detail. Before the two matches were played he had flown to Europe to watch Poland in a friendly against Bulgaria and had returned with the special make of black-and-white patterned ball that the Poles used.

Diplomatically, when agreeing to replace Ian McColl, he had hoped "for better breaks" than the man he was superseding.

Robert Kelly was supportive but, not unnaturally, supportive within limits. It was perfectly reasonable that the club should wish to be the recipients of the new manager's major endeavours. In August 1965 therefore, Celtic agreed that Stein should remain in charge of the Scotland side for the rest of the qualifying matches but on the following three clearly defined conditions:

(a) Wherever a conflict of interest arose, the club must come first.

(b) There would be no scouting. This also recognised the continuing function of the Selection Committee.

(c) There would be no future approach from the SFA for his services in a similar capacity.

On this basis Stein stayed in touch with the Scottish side through the summer and early autumn of 1965, somehow finding time to coax Celtic back from the shakiest of starts in the League Cup and take them to the final of that competition. Within a space of four weeks in October and November, he was involved in three dramatic matches at Hampden which typified the capricious swings of footballing fortunes.

In the first of them Scotland played a Polish side which had managed to lose to the persevering but untalented Finns, thereby greatly increasing Scotland's hopes of qualifying. An early captain's goal from Billy McNeill and the incessant baying of a six-figure crowd took the Scots to within seven minutes of victory when defensive slackness allowed the menacing Liberda to equalise. As the crowd began to voice its anger at a point dropped, the Poles struck again, Sadek scoring with a shot which Bill Brown, the Scots keeper, must have been unhappy at failing to save.

Scotland were now struggling but at club level Stein had considerable success two weeks later when in the League Cup Celtic defeated Rangers 2-1 and were awarded two penalties in the process, an occurrence which for the time deprived the supporters of their customary satisfaction in ascribing malign influences to the refereeing of 'Old Firm' matches.

In the World Cup, all now hinged on the return game with Italy. The match at Hampden was one of the most dramatic ever seen on that ground. Against a Scotland side that pounded remorselessly at goal, and unimaginatively for most of the time, the Italians offered their customary chillingly intellectual defence. Indeed on rare visits from their own half they looked the more likely to score and John Greig had two goal-line clearances when a limping Brown in goal had been outwitted. Then with the referee drawing breath to whistle for time Scotland surged forward in desperation. Greig and Baxter interpassed and the former drove the ball into the net. It was a courageous win and a wonderful introduction to international football for Bobby Murdoch of Celtic and Ronnie McKinnon of Rangers, but Stein was not deceived. He knew perfectly well that what was good enough at Hampden, where a huge partisan crowd ensured that doubtful decisions would go Scotland's way, would not begin to do in Italy. He had a month to get things right.

His problems were compounded, in a pleasant way, by a sparkling 4-1 win against Wales at the end of November, again at Hampden. This was one of the best Scottish displays for years and Murdoch struck up an immediate *rapport* with the debutant Charlie Cooke of Dundee. But

The best in Britain — As early as 1966 Stein was so regarded. The award is the Westclox Trophy given in recognition of Stein's efforts in season 1965-66 when Celtic won the Scottish League and League Cup, were Scottish Cup finalists and reached the semi-finals of the European Cup Winners Cup.

there his good fortune ran out, and without it there was no hope of winning in Italy or even securing the draw that would mean a play-off.

Just before the match with Italy at Hampden, Stein had in an aside thanked "the selectors who have worked so hard since last Sunday". Most of his hearers took this to be ironical and perhaps it was. Yet the selectors had moved. They had paid £100 bonus for the win at Hampden and, appalled, nodded dumbly as Stein extorted £250 a head as the price of victory in Italy. Three-figure bonuses were unheard of in British international football at that time. More, the Scottish League agreed to the cancellation on the Saturday preceding the match of those games where one of the competing sides had more than one internationalist involved.

What could not be controlled was the Anglo-Scottish dimension. A planned weekend at Largs became farcical as one by one those Scots with Football League clubs were recalled. Stein watched them go resignedly. He was a club manager himself, after all, and he knew who paid the wages, but the risk of injury was great and the planned build-up destroyed. His statement of 1 December that the Scots would not go on the defensive in Italy began to seem implausible.

Even before the Saturday afternoon he knew that he had lost Brown in goal and McNeill from central defence and in the course of that afternoon Denis Law and Billy Stevenson were removed from contention. Baxter, a player of European calibre, was already out of the party which set off for Italy composed of the makeshift and the walking wounded. A despairing eleventh-hour sortie to England had secured Adam Blacklaw, a competent goalkeeper from Burnley, and at least Willie Henderson was fit to travel.

But not to play. A few hours before kick-off the little Rangers winger declared himself unfit and although Stein's public demeanour was one of grim stoicism he must privately have despaired. With the players denied to him — Crerand, Stevenson, Mackay, Baxter, Law, St John, Henderson, Gilzean, Willie Johnston — he might almost have won the World Cup itself. The side which staggered onto the field in Naples (the Italians had switched from Rome as years later the Spaniards were to switch from Madrid) was almost bizarre in composition, so few were his options. It is worth quoting in full because it is doubtful if more than six were his first choice for the positions in which they played. The side read: Blacklaw (Burnley); Provan (Rangers), McCreadie (Chelsea), Murdoch (Celtic), McKinnon, Greig, Forrest (Rangers), Bremner (Leeds Utd), Yeats (Liverpool), Cooke (Dundee), Hughes (Celtic).

Two memories of the match remain. The first is a pre-game quote from the manager when he said, "We brought in Cooke for the Welsh game and he played so well that I can't see the selectors leaving him out of this one". This is a very interesting revelation of where nominal power, at least, still lay. Jock was quietly warning off the selectors but going through them to do it. The second memory is the sight of the gigantic Ron Yeats trotting to the centre circle to kick off, then lumbering back to shore up the Scottish defence.

The battle plan was all too simple — kick the ball anywhere for 90 minutes to gain the play-off which must bring about the ability to field a stronger side. It was the most forlorn of hopes. The Scottish genius has never been suited to clinical, intelligent defence and with an involuntary 6-2-2 formation Scotland's chances of hitting on the break were nil. One goal would do it for the Italians.

The Scots did very well to deny the Italians until just before half-time but once Pascutti had given Italy the lead there was no possibility of recovery. Yeats pushed forward to where a number nine jersey should be but the Italians flooded through the gaps and before the match ended had scored twice more. The goals were, in a sense, superfluous.

The Liverpool manager Bill Shankly, in one of his more mystic utterances, compared the Italian defence to a "forest of trees". There is, given the subsequent industrial history of Scotland, an interesting sidelight on the match. It was televised live and created great excitement in Scotland. In Greenock the shipyard, Scott's, had 50% absenteeism and had to close in the afternoon. So too had Rootes, the car factory at Linwood, where 150 key men absented themselves, while at John Brown's shipyard in Clydebank 700 men stayed away and the management warned of penalty clauses if work fell further behind on a Swedish liner.

For Stein his time in charge of the international squad had been a searing experience. He had had his fill of working with amateurs and against the all-powerful influence of the Football League. On the day after the match the *Glasgow Herald* pleaded for the abolition of the Selection Committee and the appointment of a manager who would exercise control. It would be many years before the urge to manage the national side stirred again and the money would have to be good. "Not for £10,000," he muttered in the wake of the Naples fiasco.

He had certainly done his own career no harm. Few were disposed to blame him for the shortcomings of the system and of the selectors — on the contrary there was widespread recognition that no one else would have taken Scotland to within one game of qualifying for the finals in England in the summer of 1966. The Celtic Board would have been less than human if a little relief had not been mixed in with their disappointment with the national fortunes. The job that remained to be done at Parkhead would tax all the energies of the new manager.

9

1967: ZENITH AND NADIR

THIS was to be the greatest of all Celtic's years, even if for a few brief weeks it would seem the most wretched. In the season which ended in June 1967 the team under Stein won everything that was up for competition in Scotland and became the first British club to take the major honour of all, the European Cup. They did it with a breathtaking mixture of skill, fitness, self-confidence and a curious naïve innocence — in Jim Craig's words that 'natural gallusness' of the Glaswegian.

It is well worth examining in detail Stein's approach to this season in Europe, bearing in mind that he had already considerable experience there with Dunfermline. He had all the authority of a man who had been involved in the defeat of Everton and the trouncing of Valencia. When, therefore, Stein, in almost a throw-away line, declared that he thought that Celtic were capable of winning the European Cup at their first time of entry it was not an opinion to be lightly disregarded, however fanciful it seemed. He was after all speaking of a side which against Liverpool the year before had been within touching distance of a place in the European Cup Winners' Cup Final.

Stein's handling of the European Cup run in season 1966-67 and his masterly deployment of resources will stand for all time as one of the classics of football management. The preliminary tie gave him his first break. Celtic were drawn against Zurich, an acceptable pairing since Swiss football was not highly regarded and the first leg of the tie was to be played at home. Even so, a 2-0 win was not an outstanding performance, although the manager was among the first to realise that in such situations it was a much more advantageous scoreline than 3-1 would have been.

Managers are wont to intone, almost in the manner of Gregorian chant, "we respect them as we respect all our opponents" when talking of other sides. It is a propitiatory phrase which, should defeat follow, is meant to absolve the manager from the sin of underestimation. Stein knew that Zurich were not anything like as good a side as Celtic but he also knew that in European competition it was perfectly possible to lose to inferior sides through an excess of caution. He would therefore attack in the return game in Switzerland, although the accepted wisdom in away legs was to defend. He removed temptation from his own path by deliberately including both Lennox and Chalmers, out-and-out attackers who had not hitherto figured together with great frequency in European matches. Boldness was rewarded with a 3-0 win, with Gemmell, who had scored in the first match, netting twice in Zurich, once from the penalty spot. Chalmers scored the third goal.

The awaited draw for the first round proper brought the French side, Nantes, as opponents. Again this was a good draw as it avoided Latin countries, where there were likely to be serious differences of interpretation of the laws, while it also spared Celtic the transport difficulties which would have followed had an Iron Curtain team required to be met. Celtic were calm and composed in France and a 3-1 win effectively put the tie beyond the reach of the Frenchmen. The scoreline was repeated in Glasgow but a damaging blow was the injury immediately afterwards to Joe McBride, one of the scorers.

McBride, Stein's first major signing, had been having a wonderful second season at Parkhead. By early December, with the season less than half gone, he had scored 37 goals and all kinds of scoring records seemed to be his for the taking until knee trouble struck him. His presence was crucial to Celtic but in fact he was never to regain complete fitness or his first-team place on a regular basis. Stein now demonstrated his remarkable capacity for having someone in mind to fill a specialist vacancy. He also demonstrated his even more remarkable capacity for persuading those who should have been his competitors to transfer star players to him. He moved to take Willie Wallace from Hearts while Rangers, who were also very interested, were playing abroad in Germany.

The move was brilliantly succesful. Wallace would be available for the quarter-finals of the European Cup in the spring but he needed no settling-in period in domestic competition. Right from the start he scored goals (his final tally was 21 in half a season) and his quick, darting style fitted in beautifully with that of his new colleagues.

The quarter-finals brought a longer journey to Yugoslavia to play against Vojvodina and this was to be the only match that Celtic lost in the tournament. The margin could not have been slimmer, 1-0, but Stein was concerned that Celtic had failed to score. He was even more concerned as the minutes ticked away in the return at Parkhead and the Celtic attacks dashed themselves vainly on the grimly imperturbable Slav defence.

In the end, simple human error succeeded where art and effort had not. The Yugoslav goalkeeper, Pantelic, dropped a cross ball which he would normally have swallowed and Chalmers prodded it over the line. Even then an unwanted play-off loomed, the last thing needed in a tight league situation. In a last convulsive effort, Celtic forced a corner on the right. The elegant Charlie Gallagher, a beautiful striker of the ball, took it. Billy McNeill started running from the edge of the box and the principal actors in the 1965 Scottish Cup winning goal had done it again.

Now other people besides Stein began to believe that Celtic could win the European Cup but very few of them were English. How *could* Celtic succeed where such as Manchester United and Tottenham Hotspur had failed? The attitude of Ken Jones, writing in the London edition of the *Daily Mirror* on 10 March 1967 was a fair sample of the reaction of English journalists: ". . . I should hate to be in Glasgow — the Celtic sector of it that is — on the night when dreams are broken. Because for all their support and belief, I do not regard Celtic as good enough to achieve what has proved beyond others in Britain. Persistence as much as anything brought them success against the Slavs and even their most loyal followers must recognise the luck that was delivered to their door."

Understandably, Stein did not see things in this light. More than most, he believed that the course of a game ran 90 minutes and that there was nothing fortuitous about the constantly exerted pressure which would eventually crack opponents, however late in the day.

Semi-finals of major competitions are traditionally the most hag-ridden stage. Even defeated finalists have been at the centre of things but to go out at the previous round means a comparatively drab undoing of a season's work. Once again the opponents were Slav, the Army side, Dukla Prague, from Czechoslovakia. At the end of the home tie it was hard to say if Celtic had done enough. They had taken the lead, lost it before half-time and were indebted to Wallace for two second-half goals. They led 3-1 but, very importantly, the Czechs had scored away from home.

At this point, Stein's courage and natural instincts failed him. The final was desperately near, He compromised his principles and sent out a totally defensive formation in Prague, with Steve Chalmers cast as a forlorn hope up front. It was not a pattern which suited the natural genius of the side but Stein attempted to justify it afterwards in a very odd quote which he gave to the *Celtic View*: "Our players very quickly decided that Dukla were going to be aggressive and bold and our answer was to concentrate on defence. We had not intended to be so defensively minded but in the circumstances we had no hesitation in deciding as we did." What is strange about this quotation is the apparent note of surprise that a team already 3-1 down should attack vigorously when even the layman would feel that there was no other option open to them.

The desperate defence got a 0-0 draw and although it was depressing to watch and Robert Kelly hated it, it had succeeded and Celtic were through to the final. They were where no British team had gone before them.

Jock Stein could now give free rein to his deeply felt footballing philosophy and in the following two comments, each made just before the final, the man is baring his soul: "Inter have a clear advantage of course in that they have considerable experience of the great occasions of Europe. We are only beginning to get to know them. Next Thursday night will make us much richer in experience and, who knows, champions of Europe also."

The second statement illustrates the extraordinary gift that Stein had for finding words that were as dignified and moving as the occasion itself. He never said anything finer than this: "If it should happen that we lose to Inter Milan, we want to be remembered on the Continent (and indeed all over the world because of the TV public) because of the football we played. We want to make neutrals everywhere glad that we qualified."

In the final Celtic were to have the priceless advantage of innocence, an advantage which Feyenoord of Holland would use against them three years later. Inter Milan were battle-hardened to European competition, yet from the arrival of the two sides in Portugal it was the Italians who ran scared. Their camp was barred and unwelcoming while the Celtic hotel was under siege from their exuberant fans who quickly captivated the citizens of Lisbon with their essential good humour.

Stein, apparently quite unperturbed, was able to keep the minds of his players on the task in hand while dealing urbanely and satisfactorily

Training can (sometimes) be fun — Stein is caught in a mood of high appreciation of Charlie Gallagher's ball control. Sharing his admiration are (left to right), Steve Chalmers, a very young George Connelly, Bobby Murdoch and Ian Young.

with the world's press. He had impressed on his players the need for style, "bags of swank" in the old RSM's phrase, and he had the men to deliver it.

The nerves that existed were merely those that come from the tense desire of the athlete to be off and going. Simpson's gaunt features always appeared to be racked with anxiety as he paced his goal but this was deceptive. He was coolness itself under pressure. McNeill could be relied upon to be his usual imperious self, Johnstone would see the match as a showcase, while in Gemmell and Auld, Stein had two men who would have settled a regiment.

There is a photograph of the Rangers and Celtic sides coming down the tunnel at Hampden Park just before the Scottish Cup Final of 1969. The captains, Greig and McNeill, are taut-faced. John Fallon of Celtic is keyed to a high pitch of nervousness as is Alex Ferguson of Rangers, but further back in the Celtic line is Tommy Gemmell giving a carefree wave to someone in the crowd. His insouciance was of untold value in big matches — his immediate opponent could turn him inside-out without in any way affecting Gemmell's estimation of himself as the best left-back in Europe.

On this day of days, the teams lined up as follows:

Celtic: Simpson; Young, Gemmell, Murdoch, McNeill, Clark, Johnstone, Wallace, Chalmers, Auld, Lennox.
Inter Milan: Sarti; Burgnich, Fachetti, Bedin, Guarneri, Pichi, Bicicli, Mazzola, Capellini, Corso, Domenghini.
Referee: K. Tsenscher (West Germany).

Everyone of an age to do so can remember the exact circumstances in which he or she saw the match. My own experience was to see it in the studios of Scottish Television in Glasgow where I was hosting the half-time and full-time discussion. With part of one's mind on that segment of the programme to come, it took several re-screenings of the match before it could be realised just how skilfully Celtic had gone about their task. The fire and the passion, these were appreciated immediately, but the artistry took some time to register.

The Italians had built their game on containment, *catenaccio*, and infrequent but lethal breakouts. It was not exhilarating to watch but Inter had perfected the system. To lose an early goal to them was almost certainly to lose the game and Celtic lost that early goal. Capellini was brought down in the penalty area and referee Tsenscher, correctly disregarding Celtic's protests, which were no more than ritualistic, gave the award. The penalty kick was stroked in by Mazzola with the minimum of fuss as Ronnie Simpson gambled on direction and lost.

Celtic countered down the wings, using the blistering pace of Lennox while Johnstone jinked like a swift. Inter held. Gemmell and Auld each struck the crossbar. In the Italian goal, Sarti repeatedly demonstrated his excellence. Inter held and held until half-time.

During the break, Stein moved among his players, assuring them that they had the winning of the game, urging Craig and Auld to go wide and

The Cup comes home to Paradise — The victors of Lisbon 1967 do a lorry lap of honour with the European Cup held aloft.

roll the ball back for the fearsome shooting of Gemmell and Murdoch. And still Inter held. Sarti had a miraculous smother of a Chalmers shot right on the goal-line. Celtic made a vehement claim that the ball had crossed the line but the referee again was right and the Italians kept the lead.

Still Celtic persisted, trying moves, discarding them, but in no frenzied way. It was rather a methodical examination of their own repertoire. They resisted the besetting sin of British clubs in such situations, the forlorn hoisting of hope-for-the-best high crosses, and they allowed Inter Milan absolutely no respite. At the other end goalkeeper Ronnie Simpson was every bit as much a spectator as the paying customers.

Fittingly, when the equalising goal arrived it came as Jock Stein said it would. Murdoch put Craig in possession on the right. The Inter Milan defence fell back to await the cross, but Craig, seeing Gemmell galloping up, laid the ball as if in a groove across the 18-yard line. Not even so talented and brave a goalkeeper as Sarti could do anything about Gemmell's blazing shot. Celtic were level and would now win. Inter Milan had nothing left. Essentially negative, they had no strategy but to attempt to live for another day and they got within six minutes of doing it.

As if to demonstrate that association football is after all an inexact science, the winner came from a classic movement that misfired. This time Murdoch made the running and Murdoch should have been the executioner. On the latter's own admission he hopelessly mishit his shot which was trundling harmlessly towards goal when Steve Chalmers got the merest touch to it — in cricketing terms, an outside edge. It was enough to wrongfoot Sarti and to make Celtic champions of Europe. In the few remaining minutes of play, the Italians never threatened. Herrera slipped away, glum and out-thought. So too at the very last did Stein, perhaps overcome by the magnitude of his own achievement.

The dressing-room scenes that followed are common currency. Footballers in victory are often tediously predictable, their radio and television interviews even more so but this was a team entitled to rejoice. Only one manager of an English side had the magnanimity to attend and he was a Scot. In the moment of triumph Bill Shankly delivered what most people would regard as Stein's epitaph. "John, you're immortal."

Jimmy Gordon, soon to produce the film *The Celtic Story* and much later to become the managing director of Radio Clyde, remembers a more pessimistic comment. When he congratulated the Celtic manager on an absolutely wonderful result Stein grunted and only half in jest wondered what he would be expected to do the following season. There spoke the melancholy professional, a man who knew that in association football there are very few amicable partings of the ways for managers. In the next few months his professionalism would be severely strained for news had come through that Racing Club of Argentina were the club champions of South America and their meetings with Celtic would decide the club championship of the entire footballing world.

There have been few grimmer periods in the long history of the Celtic Football Club than the three weeks which followed the first of their three matches in the World Cup Championship against Racing Club of Buenos Aires.

The seeds of disaster were already there if the eyesight was keen enough. The competition, officially designated the Inter Continental Cup and played between the club champions of Europe and their counterparts of South America had hitherto been contested exclusively by Latin countries. Thus, Portuguese had played Uruguayans and later Brazilians, Argentinians had played Italians as had also Brazilians. These games had been physical enough but at least the skulduggery was of a common brand. A Northern European side such as Celtic would be bound to be seen as robust and overheartily physical, whereas Argentinian fouls would be characterised by the Scots as sly and cowardly.

The man who made it possible — Jimmy Gribben, the Celtic scout who remembered Stein and suggested him to Celtic, sees his recommendation pay off.

There was another complication and that was the lack of recognition extended by FIFA and UEFA to what they considered a purely unofficial competition. They had taken this attitude because the organisers of the competition had not bothered to submit their curiously complicated regulations for official approval. FIFA was therefore very unlikely to intervene in the conduct of a competition which so far as it was concerned had no official existence. In previous years South American sides, notably Fluminense and Flamengo of Brazil had created a good impression in Scotland but they had not played in competitive matches.

The possibilities of trouble appeared much more starkly after the first match played at Hampden on 18 October 1967, Parkhead being out of commission because of ground reconstruction. The teams took the field to an anticipatory roar from 90,000 spectators.

Celtic: Simpson; Craig, Gemmell, Murdoch, McNeill, Clark, Johnstone, Lennox, Wallace, Auld, Hughes.
Racing Club: Carrizo; Perfumo, Diaz, Martin, Zasile, Charay, Martinoli, Rulli, Cardenas, Rodriguez, Maschio.
Referee: Juan Gardeazabal (Spain).

Celtic showed one change in personnel from the Lisbon final, Hughes playing instead of Chalmers, and right from the outset the match took on the pattern which was to characterise the three games. Celtic attacked with total commitment but were impeded, literally impeded by the Argentinians, elegant in their sky-blue and white stripes and black shorts. None suffered more than Johnstone. Where they could, the South American defenders simply ran into him and obstructed him. When that failed, the little winger was felled. Punches on the blind side and tugging of jerseys in the penalty area were the stock in trade of Racing Club. Their utter cynicism baffled Stein even more than it angered him, because he was at heart a pure football romantic and found it impossible to reconcile such tactics with the Argentinian's undoubted ability. The situation was by no means improved by the Spanish referee, Senor Juan Gardeazabal, who flapped his arms amiably and weakly while doing nothing to restore order.

As so often before in major matches, Billy McNeill came up to head the winning goal from a John Hughes corner kick but the successful efforts of the Racing defence to break up the rhythm of Celtic's attack by any means available ensured that this would be the only score.

Even at this stage, the more perceptive Celtic supporters were for pulling out of the return match. If this was how the Argentinian side comported itself before an intimidating crowd at Hampden, what would they be like back in Buenos Aires? These misgivings were abundantly shared, in private, by chairman Robert Kelly but not by the manager. The attraction of having the best club side in the world was

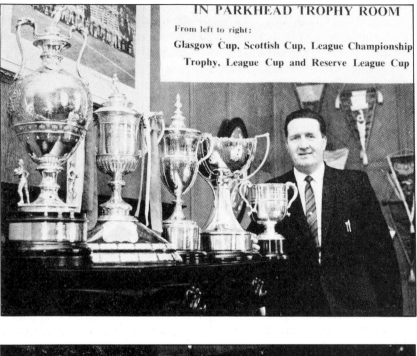

IN PARKHEAD TROPHY ROOM

From left to right:

Glasgow Cup, Scottish Cup, League Championship Trophy, League Cup and Reserve League Cup

We did it — In a moment of relief after the European Cup Final in Lisbon in 1967 Stein salutes the most prestigious trophy in Europe, never before won by a British side.

understandably strong and so the team flew out to play the return match. In so doing they would cross the equator and play in the southern hemisphere for the first time in the club's history.

Feeling in Argentina had been very anti-English since the events of the World Cup of 1966 which led to the ordering-off of the Argentinian skipper Rattin and the castigation of the national side as "animals" by Sir Alf Ramsey. On the way out to Buenos Aires there was optimistic talk that the Scots might be welcome where the English were not but this was a pitiful delusion. The distinction between Scotland and England is not one which South Americans make . . . or many North Americans for that matter. The ordinary football follower in Argentina, convinced that Rattin had been unjustly sent off at Wembley to clear the way for an English victory, was in vengeful mood. He had not forgotten the implacable hostility of Ramsey which had led him to forbid his own players to swap shirts with their opponents after the game in what had become the customary fashion. Celtic would pay a heavy price for this smouldering anger.

At the very outset of the second game there was a moment when Celtic could, with every justification, have withdrawn from any further participation in the competition. During the warm-up before the game the Celtic goalkeeper, Ronnie Simpson, was seen to fall to the ground and investigation revealed that his head had been split open by a missile presumed to have come from the crowd. He was clearly unfit to play and eventually Jock Stein, cut off from his directors by almost the length of the stadium, gave the signal to John Fallon to strip for action. Fallon, a much-criticised goalkeeper in his time, was courage exemplified that day. Never knowing but what he might be the target of a second projectile he played bravely and well. Indeed in the circumstances the whole side performed most creditably in going down only by 2-1.

Celtic had taken the lead through a Gemmell penalty awarded when the goalkeeper rugby-tackled Jimmy Johnstone. Even in Buenos Aires that was a penalty but now the Uruguayan referee, Esteban Marino, began to apply the law of compensation. The equalising goal from Rafo was widely regarded as offside although there was nothing wrong with the winner which Cardenas scored just after half-time. The sides had now won one game each and were level on goals. By the bizarre rules of this bizarre competition, they had to meet again in South America within 72 hours on neutral ground.

Robert Kelly was convinced that this third game should not take place. Two matches had been played, each side had won, Celtic had come to South America so there could be no haggle over gate money or imputations of cowardice. Stein button-holed the other directors and persuaded them to reconvene. From the resumed meeting the chairman emerged, shaking his head and muttering, "Against my better judgement".

Stein afterwards gave his reasons for wishing the third game to go ahead. "I was one of several people who pointed out that if we didn't play we might be accused of cowardice. We were, I thought, bound to get fairer treatment in a neutral country and I felt that there was some good in everybody."

These sentiments, though commendable, were sadly mistaken. Montevideo, the capital city of Uruguay, was a neutral venue in name only and tens of thousands of Argentinians swarmed across the River Plate. In this, the third match, Celtic, provoked beyond endurance, were to lose their discipline totally. In so doing they lost the chance to win over the Uruguayan section of the crowd which was not particularly well disposed towards Racing. There had been a rather naïve attempt to do this before the match when Celtic paraded under a Uruguayan flag but the Argentinians, past masters against novices in this kind of rough-house, had paraded with an earlier and larger flag.

The third match started quietly enough and midway through the first half there was some cause to hope that the bad feeling had been purged and that this might come to resemble a normal game of football. Then Johnstone, appallingly fouled yet again, blatantly elbowed his opponent and as so often happens the retaliator was dismissed while the initial offender escaped unpunished. Much worse was to follow, for within minutes the Paraguayan referee, who achieved the rare distinction of being more ineffective than Juan Gardeazabal, had sent Bobby Lennox from the field of play. Lennox was renowned for his good conduct on the field. He was in fact one of the most sportsmenlike men ever to play professional football, and the foul for which he left the field had been committed by another Celtic player, as television recordings and after-match enquiries established. In sending Lennox off, the referee, Dr Rodolfo Perez Osorio, had totally lost control and when he added John Hughes to the list of dismissals, the match became total farce. Even then the Argentinians had to struggle through to a 1-0 victory when their best forward, Cardenas, eventually pierced the depleted defence.

The last few minutes were a nightmare. Perez Osorio compounded a dismal display of refereeing by failing to dismiss Auld and Gemmell for conduct which abundantly merited dismissal. There was some confusion in the case of Auld, the referee claiming to have dismissed him. The secretary of the SFA, Willie Allan, in an excellent summation of the shambles allowed himself the wry phrase, "Auld had been sent off, but the player stayed on, apparently misunderstanding the referee's order to leave".

The secretary of the SFA's report censured the referee severely, drawing attention to glaring inconsistencies in his application of the laws. At the same time he readily conceded that at the very end Celtic behaved badly. He made two constructive recommendations. The first was that clubs should not be asked to play three matches within such a short time span. The second was that if each side won a match, the trophy should be jointly held. To avoid this happening too often there was a further recommendation that, as in the major European competitions, away goals should henceforth count double.

The on-field anarchy had momentarily shattered Stein but he recovered quickly and typically did not hide from the consequences of his own actions. He frankly avowed that he had misread the situation. "We don't run away from the incidents late in the Montevideo game. They don't show us in a good light. I am disappointed that we descended to misconduct and thereby lost dignity. The chairman was strongly of the opinion that there should be no third game. He was more concerned with the safety of the players and the right of the Celtic supporters at home to see a team unaffected by serious injury. Mr Kelly was swayed by our arguments and I now have to say that he was correct in the first place."

Humiliated and chastened as they were, acutely conscious of their own shortcomings and fall from grace Celtic were nevertheless greatly angered by the BBC television coverage which followed. It could fairly be described as a collage of Celtic fouls in the third game and Stein very justifiably pointed out that events in all three games needed to be taken into consideration. It jaundiced his attitude towards television for some considerable time and he was not alone in feeling that there were those in the English media who were not at all ill-pleased to get back at the upstarts who had had the effrontery to win the European Cup.

Of Robert Kelly it could truly be said that to him the reputation of his club was beyond rubies. Players had transgressed, therefore players must be punished. Each of them was fined £250, a decision which carried an element of unfairness in that John Fallon at least had been blameless in goal. There were other consequences. Auld and Hughes were fined £50 by the SFA and Jimmy Johnstone, whose SFA suspension had been lifted to allow him to play, more properly deferred to allow him to play, was severely censured by the same body which had shown him that indulgence.

Perhaps the strangest part of the whole proceedings is that Robert Kelly should have fought down his doubts after the first game and allowed his mind to be changed after the second. He was not noted as a man to shrink from unpalatable decisions or as a man who was often persuaded against his better judgement. He may have come to feel that he had been gainsaid on a matter which was properly the decision of the Board of directors, and the last analysis, his own. At all events, when the decision was taken not to play against any Warsaw Pact country in European competition in the wake of the Russian invasion of Czechoslovakia in 1968, the chairman made all the running and very

95

definitely spoke for the club. South America had been a bad experience. Celtic had faltered at the last hurdle but in 1970 Jock Stein would be again within reach of becoming, officially, the most successful club manager in the world.

10

SEMI-FINALS DON'T WIN TROPHIES

IN the month of April 1970 Stein and his players seemed poised to repeat their achievement of 1967 and win once again the domestic treble, Scottish League, Scottish Cup and League Cup, and the European Cup. The League Cup was already once more on the Parkhead sideboard, a gallant St Johnstone side having been defeated as far back as October. The league had been won in a canter with Rangers toiling twelve points behind. In the path of the victorious Celts lay Aberdeen in the domestic cup final and Feyenoord of Holland in the major European event. Celtic were strong favourites in both competitions but within a month the season had ended in double failure which brought a welter of recriminations and for the first time since Stein's arrival at Parkhead cast serious doubts on his judgement.

The European campaign had started in Switzerland as it had done in 1967 — a good omen, thought those who took account of such things. This time the opposition was Basle rather than Zurich and with a view to the future, it was perhaps more interesting that Danny McGrain and Kenny Dalglish went along to gain experience than that the team sheet included eight players who had been successful in Lisbon three years before. A goalless draw was a sufficiently satisfactory start to the attempt on the trophy although in European terms 1-1 would have been better. It could be dangerous if the Swiss managed to score in the return at Parkhead. In the event they did not do so and Celtic came through comfortably with goals by Hood and Gemmell.

The next team that Celtic would be required to meet were Benfica of Lisbon, still widely regarded as one of the great European sides but by then well past their best. They still had named and famed players such as Carlos Humberto, Simoes, Torres and the great Eusebio, so that Celtic were entitled to be legitimately proud of a 3-0 win in the first leg at Parkhead. Wallace and Hood had scored, so too that prolific scorer in European matches Tommy Gemmell. Stein was particularly pleased with Gemmell's goal because he had resisted the temptation to keep him out of the side at a time when relations between the two men were stormy. Gemmell was in fact going through a turbulent time. He had been left out of the League Cup Final side against St Johnstone and had put in a transfer request, the first such to come from an established first team player during Stein's four and a half years at Parkhead. He was also in bad odour with the national selectors soon afterwards when he was sent from the field against West Germany in a World Cup match in Hamburg. He was however a prolific scorer in European matches and the manager was not going to remove his own nose to spite his face.

The return to Lisbon for the second leg was a time for reminiscing, the more so that the match seemed all over — Benfica could hardly score four. Stein made the usual cautionary noises: "It took our best football of the season to produce those three goals. We're not going out there to throw it away by being too clever. It would be sheer folly to show off."

Celtic were not given the chance to show off, they were forced back into defence by a confident, poised Benfica side and by half-time their three-goal lead had been cut by two. But for an injury to Eusebio which prevented him resuming after half-time it is very doubtful if Celtic would have returned to Scotland still with an interest in the European Cup. As it was Benfica got the third goal which took matters into extra time and Celtic had to go through the nervous moments of hoping that a tossed coin would land right way up.

Stein was not amused about a match which had seen a winning lead totally disappear. "We were careless, almost unprofessional in our approach to this game" was his verdict. Still, he now had the winter break from Europe to get matters right and the enthusiasm of the support for these big matches was far from sated. When tickets went on sale for the next round against Fiorentina 40,000 were sold in a 90-minute period.

For the first match against the Italians the Celtic manager made one of those changes in personnel for which he was renowned. Auld, who had been out of the side, came back and the reintroduction of his calming presence in midfield was a master-stroke, reducing as it did the tendency of the home side to scurry too frenetically and by so doing, to play into the hands of the intelligent Italian defence. Auld himself scored, as did Wallace and the unfortunate Carpenetti, and the lead would have been regarded as conclusive had it not been for the events of the Benfica game. Stein left his players in no doubt that a repeat of the performance in Portugal would not be acceptable. "If we needed any warning that a three goal difference can be cancelled out we had it at Benfica. We must not be too clever, we must only be clever. We have lost games against Benfica and AC Milan because of carelessness and this must be avoided."

In Italy, Connelly and Auld were given the task of controlling the middle of the field which they did with great authority and no one was particularly bothered that the second leg was lost 1-0. Celtic had reached the semi-final stage and there they were to meet an English side who were as heavily involved in the race for honours as themselves, Leeds United. This would not only be a European Cup-tie, it was an unofficial British championship and the Celtic support, irked by having the efforts of their team constantly depreciated by English pressmen were desperate for success.

The Leeds United side could for once accurately be described as star-studded. Cooper, Bremner, Jackie Charlton, Lorimer and Giles were known from one end of Europe to the other and the Yorkshire club were poised to take over from Manchester United and the emerging Liverpool as the pre-eminent English team. No ground in Britain could have housed all the Scots who would want to see the home leg but Celtic maximised that number by moving the tie to Hampden where 134,000 people could be accommodated. Interest in the match was such that 60,000 tickets vanished almost as soon as the ticket booths opened.

Leeds United had looked league winners for most of the season and they had reached the final of the FA Cup where they awaited Chelsea. But by March they were faltering noticeably in the league and soon evidence emerged that their manager, Don Revie, was not sure of his own mind. Over a single weekend, the Easter weekend of 1970, he turned out six reserves in a match against relegation-threatened Southampton who won 3-1 and on the following Monday he played an entire reserve side against Derby County and crashed to a 4-1 defeat. By his actions he had overtly written off his side's chances in the league and Stein was in like a flash to take advantage of this weakness: "Leeds have got to show more than we have in this first leg. They must chase the game at home and their supporters won't allow them too long to score. Supporters expect victory at home. Leeds have shown us so much respect that it has cost them the league. I expect them to try to coax us to the half-way line. This is where they do most of their damage."

Not too many of the more objective Scottish reporters thought that Celtic would be equal to the task of defeating Leeds United over two matches but at Elland Road the Scots were superb. They had a flying start with a rather fortuitous George Connelly goal in the second minute but from then on they dictated the game and Connelly was most unfortunate to see a second goal disallowed on an extremely dubious offside decision by the badly positioned French referee. All the running for this non-goal had been done by Jimmy Johnstone who over the two matches was to torment the luckless Terry Cooper within an inch of his life. The little winger's confidence had been built cloud-high by Stein's pre-match talks which he constantly broke off to indicate Johnstone, saying, "This is the man who is going to destroy Leeds United". For all his brilliance Johnstone was a player who often needed "lifting" and his manager had this very much in mind.

An additional bonus was that the conduct of the travelling Celtic support had been exemplary and Stein was in high glee at the end of the game: "What more could I ask of players who played as they did tonight? I insist that this is only the first half of the tie but that does not detract from our magnificent performance."

Don Revie found graceful words in the bitterness of defeat: "It was an excellent performance by Celtic and it would be ungracious if I didn't say that they deserved to win."

The question now was could Celtic hold their lead or even augment it since Leeds United were nothing if not durable?

Before that return could take place at Hampden Celtic had played and lost the Scottish Cup Final against Aberdeen in a match where, although they had not played well, they had certainly not been fortune's darlings. They went down 3-1 and Stein was savage in his criticism of the match referee, R. H. Davidson of Airdrie. His vehemence was to earn him a £10 fine and a severe reprimand at the hands of the SFA. The clean sweep had therefore gone but the big prize was still very much attainable. Failure to beat Aberdeen had meant that it was now over 60 years since Celtic had taken the Scottish Cup on two consecutive occasions.

Every one of the 134,000 tickets for the Leeds United match was sold and a few thousand additional people found their way into Hampden Park by various illegal subterfuges. The huge Celtic support were hushed to silence by a magnificent Bremner goal early on which squared the tie and which Leeds defended with increasing desperation until half-time. Excuses were there if Leeds wanted them. Reaney had suffered a broken leg the day after the meeting of the two teams at Leeds and on the previous Saturday United had slogged out a 2-2 draw with Chelsea in the FA Cup Final where for once the Wembley pitch was a boggy, sandy disgrace. What beat Leeds was not only their own mental weariness but the inexorable Celtic pressure. The equaliser came from John Hughes, who always exerted supremacy over Jack Charlton, and there was no road back for the Yorkshire team whose sights had been set on the third game which would have taken place in their backyard at Hillsborough, Sheffield. The Leeds goalkeeper was injured in a clash with Hughes and before the stricken player, Sprake, could be replaced by Harvey, Celtic were ahead. As so often before Johnstone tore the tiring defence to shreds before rolling the ball almost casually into the path of Murdoch. The net bulged and Celtic were in the final. For the remaining minutes of the match they played increasingly at exhibition speed as their massed support became more and more ecstatic. Technically they had simply won through to the final but none of the spectators was in any doubt that he had in fact seen his side win the European Cup.

Their delight was understandable. The best team in England had been brought low over two competitive matches, but up in the stand two Dutchmen sat quietly, contemplating, considering. They had seen the havoc wrought by Jimmy Johnstone over the two matches and had come to the conclusion that no single player was capable of holding the darting winger. Genius, they decided, would require double marking.

Within 24 hours there was not a coach or flight to be had for Milan where the final would take place, but from now on things began to go seriously awry. Stein postponed a visit to Holland to run the rule over Feyenoord, saying that on this occasion it was not so vital to see them, although he did not offer an explanation of this remark. When eventually he did go over he saw Feyenoord draw 3-3 with Ajax and returned apparently unimpressed, strange in that Ajax had already given notice of intent that they would be one of the most powerful European sides and that by definition therefore a team which could hold them to a draw might be possessed of considerable ability.

Football managers are notorious exponents of the "let's take one game at a time" approach but significantly Stein was already allowing himself to think in terms of the forthcoming World Club Championship. In the immediate run-up to the final, Celtic played two matches against inferior opposition. The Highland League side Fraserburgh were beaten 7-0 in a Lifeboat Disaster Fund match and the Second Division side Stenhousemuir were thrashed 8-0 at Parkhead. These two matches were subsequently fiercely criticised as inadequate preparation but there were good precedents for them. It had been the normal practice of the great Hungarian sides of the early 1950s to prepare for an important match by scoring handfuls of goals against inferior opposition. The theory was that the goalposts were of the same dimensions in any grade of football and that the important thing was to build up the confidence of the goalscorers. The Stenhousemuir match was specifically arranged to give George Connelly a thorough warming-up. It is certain that had Celtic won in Milan the criticism would have been muted if not non-existent. Footballers have to be occupied somehow and the critics were not quick to suggest useful alternatives.

When Celtic arrived in Italy it became apparent that in a curious manner they had gone on the defensive. For their headquarters they chose an isolated complex at Varese, well out of town, and the Celtic camp became the excluding, tense place that the Inter one had been in Lisbon. Celtic had been offered the admirable training facilities of AC Milan but had turned them down on the tortuous argument that they did not want to alienate the supporters of Inter Milan. Just why the supporters of Inter would want to get behind the side which had taken the European Cup from them in 1967 was not made clear to anyone.

For all the forebodings, Celtic remained firm favourites to take the

European Cup for the second time when the teams filed out on to the turf of the San Siro Stadium. There had been those of a contrary opinion. Interestingly, referee Louis van Raven, who had officiated at the match with Benfica in Lisbon, declared that Feyenoord would beat Celtic if the two clubs should happen to meet and he further added that in his opinion Benfica had been much the more skilful team. Nearer home the Newcastle United trio of John McNamee (himself an ex-Celt), Bobby Moncur and Joe Harvey had warned that Feyenoord were an extremely skilful and talented side. In vain, the overweening expectation was that Celtic would complete a British treble since Manchester City had already won the Cup Winners' Cup and Arsenal the Fairs Cup.

The first surprise came when the teams lined up:

> *Feyenoord*: Pieters Graafland; Romeyn, Israel, Laseroms, Jansen, Van Duivenbode, Hasil, Van Hanegem, Wery, Kindvall, Moulijn.

> *Celtic*: Williams; Hay, Gemmell, Murdoch, McNeill, Brogan, Johnstone, Wallace, Hughes, Auld, Lennox.

> *Referee*: Concetto Lo Bello (Italy).

Many had hoped against hope that George Connelly would be included. Although a young player in years and experience he had an astonishing maturity and habit of command, the authority that such as Franz Beckenbauer exerted.

It was clear from the beginning that something was badly wrong. Celtic played with speed but little guile and their 4-2-4 formation left them dangerously exposed. The team, despite its speed, seemed somehow sluggish — on its heels. An early goal from Gemmell after a cleverly and quickly taken free kick should have settled them but immediately afterwards McNeill and Williams were culpably indecisive and the improbable-looking Israel equalised with a gentle looping header.

In the second half Celtic hung on grimly, with Johnstone as little in evidence this time as he had been the star attraction against Leeds. Evan Williams in goal, one of the four changes in personnel since the Lisbon final of 1967, kept his side in the game with a brave double save from Kindvall and Wery. The match dragged into extra time with Feyenoord becoming ever more dominant. It yet seemed as if Celtic might manage to hang on for a replay for which they would surely pick a different side and surely play with more conviction. Connelly had by now been introduced, not for the limping Brogan but for Auld. There were four minutes to survive.

They were not survived nor did Celtic deserve another opportunity. Kindvall burst through, partly impeded by McNeill who handled the ball in the area. Referee Lo Bello waited a couple of seconds and Kindvall, regaining control, ran on to slip the ball beyond Williams. Before the end, Hasil was two inches of wood away from a third. Celtic had lost and lost ignominiously.

Why? Stein had said all the normal things. "While we are confident of winning I can't agree with the current impression that Celtic can't be beaten. As far as I'm concerned it is a problem and it's an attitude that I don't fancy at all."

The trouble was that he had not convinced anyone else, indeed perhaps himself, that he meant what he said. In the airport chaos which followed the Celtic party came in for some abuse from their disenchanted followers. It was not that they had been defeated. Previous seasons had shown that they could accept defeat at least as well as the supporters of other clubs. It was that for the first time in the Stein era there was the suggestion that they had been short-changed.

Many of them had taken time off work, some indeed had given up their jobs with the cavalier attitude of the time, all had incurred considerable expense and there were increasingly disturbing rumours that the attention and energies of the players had not been concentrated exclusively or even mainly on the task in hand. Commendably, Stein refused to criticise his players overtly, contenting himself with the somewhat cryptic observation that "I know the reason but I am not going to criticise players in public". He denied that his players' preoccupation with financial interests had cost Celtic the European Cup.

He may well have believed this but his declarations appeared none too convincing when the very next day his own players issued a statement which was astonishingly ill-timed. They had been operating a commercial pool under the guidance of Glasgow journalist Ian Peebles and they now revealed that defeat in the European Cup Final had already cost the squad something like £40,000 in endorsements and bonuses Each player could potentially have made £10,000 from syndicated articles, pictures, and the profits from sporting mementoes which were to be sold from a caravan parked outside Celtic Park on match days.

The reaction of supporters was understandably not so much one of sympathy as of fury. Many felt that it did not matter whether Stein revealed the reason for the defeat or not, they thought they knew it. Stein had trudged from the Celtic bench, isolated, unbelieving. He admitted that Feyenoord had played well and praised their performance unstintingly. He had also taken a decision. He would proceed immediately to break up the Lisbon side: "If we had won the cup — and how we wanted to win it — we might have mistakenly taken the attitude that the present team could have gone on for ever."

Most of the present team now had to set out on a tour of Canada and the United States for which enthusiasm was to say the least lukewarm. Jim Brogan did not go, the injury sustained in Milan keeping him at home. Missing too was Jimmy Johnstone whose absence was at first attributed to his dislike of flying. Such an exemption was not universally popular with some of his team-mates who were not dedicated air travellers either and who felt little urge to undertake a taxing tour at the end of an exhausting season. As it turned out there were other implications.

On 21 May 1970 Johnstone asked for a transfer. He had asked for a substantial wage increase although he was only two years into a six-year contract. Again with a curious lack of timing, this demand was presented in the wake of a discreditable defeat in Milan. Celtic told him he could go and they imparted the same piece of information to Tommy Gemmell. By this time Gemmell had left the Celtic party in the USA and so had Stein a couple of days earlier. He had departed in the middle of a match against the Italian club Bari, obviously aware that the

No one wants to know a loser — Jock Stein isolated and thoughtful in Milan after Celtic had lost to the Dutch side Feyenoord in a match they were confidently expected to win.

Johnstone problem was brewing up. It was rumoured that he was also considering an offer from Manchester United to take over as manager.

His final instruction to assistant manager Sean Fallon before flying home was that Bertie Auld and Tommy Gemmell were not to be selected for any of the remaining tour matches. The pair got themselves in bother in Kearney, New Jersey, and were immediately sent home by Fallon in an act of considerable courage. Johnstone and Gemmell would subsequently withdraw their transfer requests but the image of the happy ship had been damaged almost irretrievably.

More important, the magical, mystical aura that surrounded Stein had gone. Hitherto his players had possessed blind faith in his ability to analyse and dissect opposing sides. Now he had failed to brief them adequately, had either failed to notice that the Austrian Hasil or Van Hanegem were world-class players or had not thought the information worth transmitting. His oddly dismissive description of the latter as a "poor man's Jim Baxter" had come home to haunt him.

Of course he would recover. Of course there would be other instances of his uncanny powers of interpretation and Celtic would again get as far as the semi-final of the European Cup. The shield of invincibility was gone however, in the same way as Robert E. Lee's misjudgement at Gettysburg removed him from the category of superhuman.

It was an unhappy time and although Ronnie Simpson's decision to retire only formalised an existing situation it was another break with successful days. In the middle of this first bad managerial period he was called to London to be invested with the CBE and even that seemed a lesser reward than it should have been.

11

NINE LEAGUES DISTANCE

IN May 1966 Celtic won the Scottish League in Stein's first full season of management. It would be May 1975 before they again had experience of being anything but champions. It was a feat unparalleled in modern times although Celtic themselves had taken six titles in a row in the very early years of the century. In the 1920s Rangers put five together and after an interruption from Motherwell took the next three, thereby becoming champions eight times in nine starts.

Rangers remained consistent in post-Second World War Scottish football whereas Celtic were inured to League failure and had but one triumph, that of 1954, to brag about. Under Stein that changed radically. The leagues were won in different ways. Some were won in a canter, some were snatched in the last minutes of the last game. For the greater part of the time Rangers were certainly the team to beat but Celtic won leagues where both matches against the Ibrox side were lost and they held off challenges from Aberdeen and Hibernian. Stein taught them consistency. There was even a consistent stutter year after year when it seemed the flag was already theirs. By a statistical quirk, the championship was won nine times on nine different grounds, none of them Parkhead. The only time it was clinched in a home game, Celtic were temporary tenants at Hampden owing to major redevelopment work at Parkhead.

In this extraordinary run of sustained success lies Stein's real claim to greatness. The feat is all the more remarkable when it is considered that the great sides normally have a period of five years at most at the top. Stein doubled this and in so doing twice almost entirely recast the personnel who were achieving it for him.

The statistics of this great run will be found as an appendix. What is more important for the moment is the scope of the operation and its execution. The notion that Rangers could be excluded from the championship of Scotland for a decade passed belief in the mid-1960s and anyone who propounded it could scarcely have complained if he found himself regarded as certifiable.

Stein's achievement was a compound of shrewd buying, clever and relentlessly applied psychological pressure and a constant fine-tuning of the side, what he called "freshening" it. It was the exception rather than the rule to find the same Celtic side fielded two weeks running. Above all, his winning method was based on non-stop aggression at a time when scoring had dried up in the Scottish game with the advent of method football. In the 306 games which comprised the nine league campaigns, no fewer than 868 goals were scored, an average of almost three a game. From the same number of matches Rangers scored 694 goals, Hibernian 603, Aberdeen 556 and Heart of Midlothian a paltry 440.

As with most other human activities, the first time was the most important. It gave a collection of talented but hitherto unsuccessful players the knowledge that the major prizes could be theirs.

1965-66

What distinguished the Celtic performance in this particular season from the immediate past was the ability to put away the weaker sides and stay in contention until the New Year period. Celtic were able to do this despite being without McNeill who had suffered one of his very few injuries. The introduction of Simpson in goal had calmed the defence wonderfully. He was more resistant to pressure than John Fallon, especially when it came from the manager. A 5-1 win over Rangers at Parkhead in the New Year's fixture was an excellent start to the second half of the league campaign and Celtic's most convincing win in an 'Old Firm' league match for many years. Yet almost immediately Celtic proceeded to cast away their hard-won advantage hand over fist. They lost at Aberdeen, at Tynecastle against Hearts in the wake of the notorious Tbilisi trip and, unforgivably, against Stirling Albion at Annfield. With eleven matches to go a comfortable lead had been transformed into a two-point deficit and an inferior goal average to that of Rangers.

The supporters, cynical, had seen it all before but Stein remained unperturbed and insisted that the Ibrox side would also have their Annfields and drop the unexpected point here and there. They did so at Falkirk and stuttered badly in the run-in so that in the end the league was won more comfortably than the two-point margin would suggest. Such wins were rare and would have been welcomed by the support even as an isolated triumph but they were to become as much a way of life for Celtic followers as summer holidays and Christmas.

1966-67

The same two clubs fought out the league championship again — Clyde, a gallant third, were never in serious contention — but this time Celtic had a point more in hand when the last match was played. The salient feature of this championship was that it was won after Stein suffered the loss of McBride just before Christmas, at a time when the stocky forward was set to threaten every Scottish goal-scoring record in existence. He had scored 37 times in less than half a season when the need for a cartilage operation curtailed his career at Parkhead. There can have been few more immediately successful replacements than the one which saw Willie Wallace brought from Hearts for £25,000 in December 1966. He had been around the Scottish senior scene for the best part of ten years and with three clubs, Stenhousemuir, Raith Rovers and Hearts, had always looked just that little bit short of being a very good player. Stein changed that, and the newcomer blossomed with fine players all around him.

Stein's commitment to all-out attack was never better exemplified than in the away games at Easter Road and Dunfermline where Celtic came through 5-3 and 5-4 with the win in Fife coming very late and very much against the collar. A bad spell around Christmas saw Rangers close the gap and the Ibrox side might well have been favourites to win the crucial New Year match at their own ground had the weather allowed it to go ahead.

This was the year of Rangers' shock dismissal from the Scottish Cup by Berwick Rangers but although that was a dreadful blow to self-esteem, it freed them to concentrate on the league, at a time when Celtic were still going for everything and surviving narrowly in Europe against Vojvodina. When the match against Rangers eventually took place — and it was May before it did — the strain should have been off but Celtic had lost before their own supporters to Dundee United who thus had the distinction of returning the double against the team which would win everything that season. It was still possible in theory to throw away the league against Rangers but a fighting 2-2 draw in the deluge was enough to be champions twice in succession.

1967-68

Football managers overwork the word "character" severely. Often they apply it to players with no great discernible talent but that of stopping anyone else from displaying it. Stein's favourite term of approval for a player was "manly". He worshipped skill but admired durability and dependability. In the same season of 1967-68 McNeill, Murdoch and Gemmell did not miss a league game and Ronnie Simpson only missed one. But that one was against Rangers and it turned what might have been a comfortable victory in the championship into a cliff-hanger.

Celtic had gone into the New Year game against Rangers at Parkhead two points behind Rangers and they came out with the margin the same. They had comprehensively outplayed the Light Blues but poor John Fallon, in goal for the day and a bag of nerves, had conceded two incredible goals which restricted Celtic to a point. Moreover, although the Ibrox club were not playing well, they displayed an admirable ability to stagger through even when struggling. There can be no more eloquent testimony to Rangers than the fact that Celtic won their last 16 games and yet, starting this marvellous run on 20 January, it was 17 April before they narrowly nosed in front — and then only on goal average.

In the last home match of the season consternation reigned when with seconds left at Parkhead Morton were holding staunchly to a 1-1 draw. The match had run into injury time; the game at Kilmarnock was over and Rangers had won there. With time almost up Lennox scrambled a goal that had Stein, in the *Glasgow Herald*'s phrase, "shooting from the dug-out like a cork to congratulate the scorer who was already under siege from his colleagues". The formalities were completed at Dunfermline a few days later and the manager's record was three out of three.

Towards the end of the season 1967-68 Celtic had applied to the Scottish League for permission to enter their reserve side as a member of the Second Division. Stein's thought was that his young players needed sterner competitive matches than the Reserve League was able to offer. Celtic pointed out that there were 19 clubs in the Second Division at this time and that their inclusion would remove the awkward

Jock Stein, Sir Robert Kelly and Billy McNeill.

situation whereby a Second Division club stood idle each week. Celtic indicated that they were well aware that there could be no question of the second eleven gaining promotion even if they should happen to win the Second Division.

There was opposition from the chairman of Partick Thistle, Tom Reid, whose club would have had to play in opposition to Celtic were the new set-up approved. Stein was quick to explain his motives. "Our decision is in no way aimed at Thistle, Clyde or anyone else. We want to help Scottish football and we feel that our move would benefit the game in Scotland."

The Scottish League did not agree and the request was refused. Apart from the danger of creating a precedent, there was every possibility that the Celtic reserve side of the time could have won the Second Division championship, which, even if they were ineligible for promotion, would have been embarrassing for all concerned. Celtic felt just a little disgruntled, remembering that some years before they had voluntarily switched to the North-Eastern section of the reserve league to keep a balance for the game and to help out the Scottish League.

1968-69

This championship, the beginning of the middle phase of the nine successive victories, was won by a comfortable five-point margin over Rangers whose challenge was faltering year by year, and success was attained that much earlier. But the victory was slightly tarnished by the fact that Rangers recorded a league double against Celtic. After each Ibrox victory the Celtic response was consistent and apparently endless. Rangers won well at Parkhead in September — only Morton would equal their feat of scoring four goals against Celtic in the entire season — but Celtic then went 16 games without defeat. In similar vein when the New Year's Day game was disappointingly lost to a John Greig penalty, Stein's team put the reverse behind them and were not beaten again for 13 matches, losing only to Morton when in truth it did not matter.

Stein had by this time perfected the idea of the squad, and beyond that the introduction of a large number of young players in dead games. Thus, after Celtic had recorded a devastating 10-0 win over Hamilton Academicals in the League Cup with Lennox and Chalmers each scoring an improbable five, the manager made no apologies for filling the side with untried players for the return match. "I know I'll be criticised for playing so many of my young players in this game. They will be pointing out my duty to field a full-strength side. It is also my duty to see that Celtic maintain a high standard and position in British football."

This use of the word "British" gives an idea of Stein's standards of performance and success. It was becoming more difficult to find stern opposition at home. Even the much recast young Celtic team won the return at Hamilton comfortably enough by 4-2. This was the season when the composition of the team began to change quickly. The Lions were moving off. Simpson played a comparative handful of games as did John Clark. Joe McBride said good-bye, Steve Chalmers played half a season and Bertie Auld considerably less than that. Into the side came Harry Hood from Clyde who should have been a Celtic player three years before but Sunderland had stepped in. Hood had much of the finesse of Charlie Gallacher but was a much more prolific goalscorer. Tom Callaghan was the other import, while of the home-grown youngsters the moody George Connelly made six appearances and Lou

At the top — Stein with captain Billy McNeill and from the trophy cupboard the Drybrough Cup, the Scottish Cup and League Cup.

Macari one. The latter was an extraordinary player in that he made a considerable impact during his time at Parkhead and yet in only one of his five seasons did he play in more than half the first-team league matches.

The players were changing but the results were constant and the raising of the league flag a permanent part of the August ritual.

1969-70

In what was more a procession than a league race Celtic finished 12 points ahead of Rangers and the only interest was in seeing if they could record a century of league goals for the fourth time in five starts under Stein. They fell short by just four goals but in truth some of the other statistics were sufficiently staggering. In five seasons of league football Celtic had dropped a mere 51 points and had lost but 14 games. The manager seemed to possess powers of necromancy. John Fallon had taken over from Ronnie Simpson in goal but was never able to convince his hard taskmaster that he was the long term answer. In one of his infrequent forays to the English market, Stein brought Evan Williams back to Scotland from Wolverhampton Wanderers and the same season saw the name of Dalglish first appear on a Celtic league team-sheet although it would be another two seasons before he burst through as a regular.

1970-71

As Celtic set out after their sixth consecutive championship Stein's threat was twofold. Rangers had for the moment dropped out of the running as league challengers — they would take barely a point a game over this particular season. Aberdeen were the team to watch but the main danger to Stein was the sense of *déja-vu* and his paramount problem was to lift his side and keep them motivated and interested.

He did this by rotating his players so that they were never entirely sure of a place, by introducing youngsters such as Danny McGrain who would clearly claim a permanent position and by quite bluntly dropping even the most established players from time to time. He was totally unrepentant. This was what the club paid him to do and it was the only way to keep them to the repetitive road of winning at Brockville on a pouring wet afternoon and of snatching a draw on an icy surface at Rugby Park.

No one was immune. Towards the end of November Jimmy Johnstone had indicated that he was not keen to play against St Mirren, stating that he was not mentally prepared — not an attitude likely to commend itself to his manager. His omission from the team against Morton three weeks later was therefore no great surprise but it was coupled with the dropping of Billy McNeill. Stein spelled it out. At a conference on Boxing Day 1970 he had this to say: "There's no big secret about it. They haven't been playing well recently and this may give them the necessary jolt at aiming to get back as quickly as possible. It has happened to many other players in the pool at Parkhead this season."

The morale of the playing staff remained sufficiently high to secure a crucial draw at Pittodrie against Aberdeen even without Auld, Gemmell, Hughes and Murdoch and despite the submission of an inaptly timed transfer request from Lou Macari. In securing the draw Celtic hung onto a two-point lead which was their margin at season's end. They also hung on to their manager. It had been an open secret that Stein was considering a move to Manchester United. With no great haste Stein now quashed the rumours while stopping short of disclosing whether he had actually been offered the job. "I'll be staying here as long as I'm needed. We've been through a lot together in the last six glorious years and you don't break links so easily."

Even an unseasonable downpour, which saw a league game called off in late April and meant three games in five days in the run-in, could not mar the final party piece when the Lisbon side assembled for one last time and in thrashing a good-natured Clyde team provided one of the genuinely emotional moments in Scottish football history.

Would continual success lose its savour, even for Celtic followers? There was some evidence that this was so. Long-term domination by one team in any sport has a depressing effect on attendances. Surrey provided a classic case of this in winning the County Championship in cricket for seven consecutive years in the 1950s. By the time of their last success their gates had slumped by an astonishing two-thirds and although attendances were falling everywhere, Surrey actually suffered a greater loss than several far less successful counties. In the year 1970-71 Scottish football lost 143,000 customers and 47,000 of them were Celtic followers.

Stein could hardly be expected to see this as a reason for rolling over and playing dead. Nor was he delighted when people accused him of winning a non-competitive league. "It's sometimes claimed that Celtic have won the Scottish League and League Cup these last few years because there was no competition. I've never believed that, because if it was true surely we would have been found out in Europe."

Of one thing he was sure. There was no salvation for the financial ills of football from sponsors. Writing in the *Celtic View* of January 1971 he delivered his opinion: "If we're looking to sponsors to save football we're looking in the wrong direction. All the rewards of sponsored football are for teams that are successful. There is no salvation there for unsuccessful teams — the teams that need help."

For the moment he did not know what it was like to be unsuccessful.

He had led yet another flag-winning team and his reserves had lifted the Reserve League Cup against Rangers on an incredible 10-2 aggregate. There seemed an endless conveyor-belt of brilliant young players and European success was round the corner. The fact that the Press had got hold of the story of his decision to stay on at Parkhead just before he could reveal it in the *Sunday Mirror* in his own column was the merest flaw to show that this was not quite a perfect world. There was no more pressing problem than whether the enclosure roof at Parkhead could take the weight of the number of flagpoles that seemed likely to be required.

1971-72

This was the season in which Stein found himself in the position of a West End impresario who wonders if a long-running success can survive an almost total change of cast. The Lisbon Lions had taken their final bow against Clyde in May 1971. It had been widely known that this would be Auld's last appearance in a Celtic jersey, but within months Gemmell, Wallace and Hughes were to find themselves in English football. The first two were indelibly associated with the great events of 1967 and while Hughes had not played at Lisbon, he was nevertheless a very senior player.

During the close season Stein had hinted at impending change. Writing in the *Celtic View* of July 1971 he addressed himself to the form of Hughes, Gemmell and Bobby Murdoch over the season just gone: "Each of them received a nasty injury last term which affected their fitness and also their playing urgency." They would be moved on, though Murdoch still had a very serviceable season and a half left at Parkhead.

The more percipient Celtic supporter might have been a trifle concerned by the composition of the reserve side which played against Rangers early in the season. It read: Marshall, Craig, McGrain, McCluskey, J. Davidson, Cattenach, Hancock, Hood, Franchetti, Wallace, Hughes. Of that eleven only McGrain, and to a lesser extent McCluskey, would come through to become regular first-team players.

The goalkeeper was the very experienced Gordon Marshall who played for both Edinburgh clubs and Newcastle United but never settled with Celtic. The manager continued to tinker with the goalkeeping position. An inglorious 4-1 defeat in the League Cup Final by Partick Thistle led to the dropping of Evan Williams and the signing of Denis Connaghan from St Mirren. That was no permanent solution either and before a year was out Alistair Hunter would be summoned from Kilmarnock to take over. Either the manager was too demanding in what he asked of his last line, or the calibre of signing was deficient.

In contrast, the signing of Dixie Deans from Motherwell for a thief's bargain was a brilliant stroke of work. Deans was working out a suspension (not his first) when the Celtic manager approached Motherwell and gave the impression that he was putting his neck on the block with his directors by showing an interest in a player with such an indifferent disciplinary record. John Deans was to come to Parkhead, behave himself pretty well and become only the second man in the entire history of Scottish football to score a hat-trick in a Scottish Cup final. Whatever his difficulties with goalkeepers, Stein's taste in strikers was impeccable, first Joe McBride, then Willie Wallace and now, Dixie Deans. The seventh consecutive league championship was taken without any strain whatsoever, Aberdeen finishing a bad second ten points behind and Rangers, in third place, were a further six points away.

1972-73

This was a much more competitive season and in the end there was only a point of difference between Celtic and the recovering Rangers. Dalglish was in his second full season and giving abundant proof that the most overworked of football terms, genius, might fairly be applied to him. McGrain too was well established and George Connelly in his fifth year of first-team football hinted at an awesome power and maturity. Lou Macari decided that his future was not with Celtic. He had a higher scoring rate and a lower basic wage than several of his colleagues and this prompted his course of action. A slight air of mystery pervaded his transfer. It had been widely expected that he would go to Liverpool but Manchester United came late on the scene and Macari's destination was Old Trafford. He was an extremely valuable acquisition to the Manchester side but Stein was reputed to be none too happy about the change of plan.

In January 1973 Stein was taken to hospital with a suspected heart attack. In his absence the team gave a spiritless display in the New Year match at Ibrox and lost to Rangers. He was discharged from the Victoria Infirmary after 12 days and spent a short time convalescing in the North of Scotland. It was almost the first time he had been posted missing, even for the shortest spell.

Over the next two months Celtic slumped in the league to the extent that they almost threw away an impregnable position. On 28 February Stein thought things sufficiently serious to write an open letter to the fans in the current issue of the *Celtic View*. They may have taken as an instance of his recovery a couple of vintage swipes at the sports press: "Our losses are received by Scottish sportswriters as 'a good result for Scottish football. It'll make for a more exciting league'." It did, but in the end Celtic rallied sufficiently to hold on by that one point.

1973-74

This last year of league success for Celtic was harder on Stein than any that had gone before. The season began badly with Hay asking for a transfer and a horrific injury to young Brian McLaughlin in the very first league match. Jimmy Johnstone was under a cloud and in the reserves while Murdoch's faithful years of service ended with his transfer to Middlesbrough. Somewhat aldermanic in outline, his passing always bore the precision of the classical Scottish wing-half.

Stein took himself off to Switzerland to watch two Peruvian prospects, Quisandira and Reyes but, ever the psychologist, the prime purpose was almost certainly to take the supporters' minds off the bad news from home rather than the serious intention of doing business with the South Americans.

The manager, who in many senses *was* the club, gave the impression of an organisation not at ease with itself. The dispute with David Hay intensified. The player stayed away from training and was suspended by the club. Celtic claimed that having put the player up for transfer and having agreed terms with another club, Hay had then wanted extra money from Celtic. The player did not accept this version but whatever the rights and wrongs of the matter the Celtic support was concerned that a popular and brave player should no longer see himself as part of the Parkhead scene.

In late November Stein formally denied the rumours which were circulating that all was not well on the staff. Such a denial had the usual effect of intensifying the gossip which was refuelled by the news that George Connelly was also missing from Parkhead. The incident was patched up and Stein announced that he had found a solution to the player's worry which was a private matter. He had not found a solution and over the next year Connelly's walk-outs became more frequent and more damaging until at last the club was constrained to let him go.

Against this unpromising background, the ninth and final championship has some claim to be regarded as Stein's finest achievement, being secured in the weeks which followed the scandalous European Cup match at Parkhead against Atletico Madrid. Celtic had been angered when, in the previous round against the Swiss club, Basle, the *Sunday Mail* had assigned their old-time adversary, Jim Baxter, to report on their European performance. Baxter was not a regular newspaper reporter and the choice of writer was felt to be somewhat gratuitous. A letter to the *Celtic View* enquired plaintively why some celebrated ex-Celt could not have been found to report on the match but such a choice would scarcely have called forth the controversy which is the staff and prop of popular newspapers.

Stein was full of forebodings of what the Atletico match might bring in its train: "I also note that six of their players are Argentinians and remembering our sad experience in 1967 in South America against their countrymen of Racing Club in the World Club Championship, I ponder a wee bit more."

The game was a kicking match with three Argentinians sent from the field although even then the depleted side held on to prevent Celtic scoring. Once more the directors came under pressure to forfeit the second leg and to stay away from Madrid. Celtic went and lost, to no one's surprise and certainly not Stein's. "We knew what would await us in Spain. Wave upon wave of hatred whipped up by a vicious press campaign founded on absolute dishonesty and hypocrisy." Stinging words coming from a man who had idolised the great Spanish players of

1965-66

		P	W	D	L	F	A	Pt.
1	Celtic	34	27	3	4	106	30	57
2	Rangers	34	25	5	4	91	29	55
3	Kilmarnock	34	20	5	9	73	46	45
4	Dunfermline	34	19	6	9	94	55	44
5	Dundee Utd.	34	19	5	10	79	51	43
6	Hibernian	34	16	6	12	81	55	38
7	Hearts	34	13	12	9	56	48	38
8	Aberdeen	34	15	6	13	61	54	36
9	Dundee	34	14	6	14	61	61	34
10	Falkirk	34	15	1	18	48	72	31
11	Clyde	34	13	4	17	62	64	30
12	Partick Th.	34	10	10	14	55	64	30
13	Motherwell	34	12	4	18	52	69	28
14	St. Johnstone	34	9	8	17	58	81	26
15	Stirling Alb.	34	9	8	17	40	68	26
16	St. Mirren	34	9	4	21	44	82	22
17	Morton	34	8	5	21	42	84	21
18	Hamilton	34	3	2	29	27	117	8

1966-67

		P	W	D	L	F	A	Pt.
1	Celtic	34	26	6	2	111	33	58
2	Rangers	34	24	7	3	92	31	55
3	Clyde	34	20	6	8	64	48	46
4	Aberdeen	34	17	8	9	72	38	42
5	Hibernian	34	19	4	11	72	49	42
6	Dundee	34	16	9	9	74	51	41
7	Kilmarnock	34	16	8	10	59	46	40
8	Dunfermline	34	14	10	10	72	52	38
9	Dundee Utd.	34	14	9	11	68	62	37
10	Motherwell	34	10	11	13	59	60	31
11	Hearts	34	11	8	15	39	48	30
12	Partick Th.	34	9	12	13	49	68	30
13	Airdrie	34	11	6	17	41	53	28
14	Falkirk	34	11	4	19	33	70	26
15	St. Johnstone	34	10	5	19	53	73	25
16	Stirling	34	5	9	20	31	85	19
17	St. Mirren	34	4	7	23	25	81	15
18	Ayr Utd.	34	1	7	26	20	86	9

1967-68

		P	W	D	L	F	A	Pt.
1	Celtic	34	30	3	1	106	24	63
2	Rangers	34	28	5	1	93	34	61
3	Hibernian	34	20	5	9	67	49	45
4	Dunfermline	34	17	5	12	64	41	39
5	Aberdeen	34	16	5	13	63	48	37
6	Morton	34	15	6	13	57	53	36
7	Kilmarnock	34	13	8	13	59	57	34
8	Clyde	34	15	4	15	55	55	34
9	Dundee	34	13	7	14	62	59	33
10	Partick Th.	34	12	7	15	51	67	31
11	Dundee Utd.	34	10	11	13	53	72	31
12	Hearts	34	13	4	17	56	61	30
13	Airdrie	34	10	9	15	45	58	29
14	St. Johnstone	34	10	7	17	43	52	27
15	Falkirk	34	7	12	15	36	50	26
16	Raith Rov.	34	9	7	18	58	86	25
17	Motherwell	34	6	7	21	40	66	19
18	Stirling Alb.	34	4	4	26	29	105	12

1968-69

		P	W	D	L	F	A	Pt.
1	Celtic	34	23	8	3	89	32	54
2	Rangers	34	21	7	6	81	32	49
3	Dunfermline	34	19	7	8	63	45	45
4	Kilmarnock	34	15	14	5	50	32	44
5	Dundee Utd.	34	17	9	8	61	49	43
6	St. Johnstone	34	16	5	13	66	59	37
7	Airdrie	34	13	11	10	46	44	37
8	Hearts	34	14	8	12	52	54	36
9	Dundee	34	10	12	12	47	48	32
10	Morton	34	12	8	14	58	68	32
11	St. Mirren	34	11	10	13	40	54	32
12	Hibernian	34	12	7	15	60	59	31
13	Clyde	34	9	13	12	35	50	31
14	Partick Th.	34	9	10	15	39	53	28
15	Aberdeen	34	9	8	17	50	59	26
16	Raith Rov.	34	8	5	21	45	67	21
17	Falkirk	34	5	8	21	33	69	18
18	Arbroath	34	5	6	23	41	82	16

1969-70

		P	W	D	L	F	A	Pt.
1	Celtic	34	27	3	4	96	33	57
2	Rangers	34	19	7	8	67	40	45
3	Hibernian	34	19	6	9	65	40	44
4	Hearts	34	13	12	9	50	36	38
5	Dundee Utd.	34	16	6	12	62	64	38
6	Dundee	34	15	6	13	49	44	36
7	Kilmarnock	34	13	10	11	62	57	36
8	Aberdeen	34	14	7	13	55	45	35
9	Dunfermline	34	15	5	14	45	45	35
10	Morton	34	13	9	12	52	52	35
11	Motherwell	34	11	10	13	49	51	32
12	Airdrie	34	12	8	14	59	64	32
13	St. Johnstone	34	11	9	14	50	62	31
14	Ayr Utd.	34	12	6	16	37	52	30
15	St. Mirren	34	8	9	17	39	54	25
16	Clyde	34	9	7	18	34	56	25
17	Raith Rov.	34	5	11	18	32	67	21
18	Partick Th.	34	5	7	22	41	82	17

1970-71

		P	W	D	L	F	A	Pt.
1	Celtic	34	25	6	3	89	23	56
2	Aberdeen	34	24	6	4	68	18	54
3	St. Johnstone	34	19	6	9	59	44	44
4	Rangers	34	16	9	9	58	34	41
5	Dundee	34	14	10	10	53	45	38
6	Dundee Utd.	34	14	8	12	53	54	36
7	Falkirk	34	13	9	12	46	53	35
8	Morton	34	13	8	13	44	44	34
9	Motherwell	34	13	8	13	43	47	34
10	Airdrie	34	13	8	13	60	65	34
11	Hearts	34	13	7	14	41	40	33
12	Hibernian	34	10	10	14	47	53	30
13	Kilmarnock	34	10	8	16	43	67	28
14	Ayr Utd.	34	9	8	17	37	54	26
15	Clyde	34	8	10	16	33	59	26
16	Dunfermline	34	6	11	17	44	56	23
17	St. Mirren	34	7	9	18	38	56	23
18	Cowdenbeath	34	7	3	24	33	77	17

15 years before, Puskas, Di Stefano and Gento, but the bitterness was heartfelt and would surface again in 1985.

The season finished with a dash of swagger, a touch of panache, when Celtic went down to Liverpool and beat the home side 4-1 in a testimonial match for Ron Yeats who had caused national heart-failure at Naples away back in 1965 by appearing to line-up in the centre-forward position before ambling back to his more usual defensive post. It was a World Cup summer, 1974, and both sides fielded weakened

1971-72

		P	W	D	L	F	A	Pt.
1	Celtic	34	28	4	2	96	28	60
2	Aberdeen	34	21	8	5	80	26	50
3	Rangers	34	21	2	11	71	38	44
4	Hibernian	34	19	6	9	62	34	44
5	Dundee	34	14	13	7	59	38	41
6	Hearts	34	13	13	8	53	49	39
7	Partick Th.	34	12	10	12	53	54	34
8	St. Johnstone	34	12	8	14	52	58	32
9	Dundee Utd.	34	12	7	15	55	70	31
10	Motherwell	34	11	7	16	49	69	29
11	Kilmarnock	34	11	6	17	49	64	28
12	Ayr Utd.	34	9	10	15	40	58	28
13	Morton	34	10	7	17	46	52	27
14	Falkirk	34	10	7	17	44	60	27
15	Airdrie	34	7	12	15	44	76	26
16	East Fife	34	5	15	14	34	61	25
17	Clyde	34	7	10	17	33	66	24
18	Dunfermline	34	7	9	18	31	50	23

1972-73

		P	W	D	L	F	A	Pt.
1	Celtic	34	26	5	3	93	28	57
2	Rangers	34	26	4	4	74	30	56
3	Hibernian	34	19	7	8	74	33	45
4	Aberdeen	34	16	11	7	61	34	43
5	Dundee	34	17	9	8	68	43	43
6	Ayr Utd.	34	16	8	10	50	51	40
7	Dundee Utd.	34	17	5	12	56	51	39
8	Motherwell	34	11	9	14	38	48	31
9	East Fife	34	11	8	15	46	54	30
10	Hearts	34	12	6	16	39	50	30
11	St. Johnstone	34	10	9	15	52	67	29
12	Morton	34	10	8	16	47	53	28
13	Partick Th.	34	10	8	16	40	53	28
14	Falkirk	34	7	12	15	38	56	26
15	Arbroath	34	9	8	17	39	63	26
16	Dumbarton	34	6	11	17	43	72	23
17	Kilmarnock	34	7	8	19	40	71	22
18	Airdrie	34	4	8	22	34	75	16

1973-74

		P	W	D	L	F	A	Pt.
1	Celtic	34	23	7	4	82	27	53
2	Hibernian	34	20	9	5	75	42	49
3	Rangers	34	21	6	7	67	34	48
4	Aberdeen	34	13	16	5	46	26	42
5	Dundee	34	16	7	11	67	48	39
6	Hearts	34	14	10	10	54	43	38
7	Ayr Utd.	34	15	8	11	44	40	38
8	Dundee Utd.	34	15	7	12	55	51	37
9	Motherwell	34	14	7	13	45	40	35
10	Dumbarton	34	11	7	16	43	58	29
11	Partick Th.	34	9	10	15	33	46	28
12	St. Johnstone	34	9	10	15	41	60	28
13	Arbroath	34	10	7	17	52	69	27
14	Morton	34	8	10	16	37	49	26
15	Clyde	34	8	9	17	29	65	25
16	Dunfermline	34	8	8	18	43	65	24
17	East Fife	34	9	6	19	26	51	24
18	Falkirk	34	4	14	16	33	58	22

POSSIBLE APPEARANCES—306

	'66	'67	'68	'69	'70	'71	'72	'73	'74	Total
B. McNeill	25	33	34	34	31	31	34	30	30	282
J. Johnstone	32	25	29	30	26	30	23	21	13	229
B. Murdoch	31	31	34	30	24	21	15	24	—	210
B. Lennox	22	26	28	27	18	22	24	15	17	199
T. Gemmell	34	34	34	31	28	19	3	—	—	183
J. Brogan	2	—	18	30	27	26	20	20	30	173
J. Craig	15	17	22	32	20	22	16	—	—	144
J. Hughes	24	19	31	27	19	15	—	—	—	135
W. Wallace	—	21	29	29	29	25	2	—	—	135
H. Hood	—	—	—	7	26	27	24	22	28	134
D. Hay	—	—	—	—	25	27	28	21	25	126
G. Connelly	—	—	—	6	7	22	32	32	14	113
T. Callaghan	—	—	—	12	12	16	28	27	16	111
R. Simpson	30	33	33	12	—	—	—	—	—	110
J. Clark	34	34	18	9	9	1	—	—	—	105
K. Dalglish	—	—	—	—	2	1	31	32	31	97
B. Auld	17	27	19	9	17	4	—	—	—	93
S. Chalmers	23	28	13	17	5	3	—	—	—	89
E. Williams	—	—	—	—	—	16	31	20	15	82
D. Deans	—	—	—	—	—	—	21	30	24	75
D. McGrain	—	—	—	—	—	—	2	30	29	61
J. McBride	31	14	4	4	—	—	—	—	—	53
L. Macari	—	—	—	1	13	8	19	10	—	51
J. Fallon	4	1	1	22	16	3	—	—	—	47
C. Gallagher	18	11	13	—	—	—	—	—	—	42
A. Hunter	—	—	—	—	—	—	15	26	—	41
P. McCluskey	—	—	—	—	—	—	2	14	23	39
S. Murray	—	—	—	—	—	—	—	32	3	35
W. O'Neill	—	—	18	6	4	—	—	—	—	28
D. Connaghan	—	—	—	—	—	—	8	14	4	26
J. Quinn	—	—	—	—	1	—	9	9	3	22
I. Young	16	1	—	—	—	—	—	—	—	17
V. Davidson	—	—	—	—	1	6	5	1	3	16
J. Cushley	12	1	—	—	—	—	—	—	—	13
D. Cattanach	1	—	4	1	—	4	—	—	—	10
J. Divers	3	—	—	—	—	—	—	—	—	3
J. Bone	—	—	—	—	—	—	—	3	—	3
F. Welsh	—	—	—	—	—	—	3	—	—	3
R. McDonald	—	—	—	—	—	—	—	2	—	2
B. McLaughlin	—	—	—	—	—	—	—	—	2	2
P. McMahon	—	—	2	—	—	—	—	—	—	2
C. Shevlane	—	—	2	—	—	—	—	—	—	2
A. Lynch	—	—	—	—	—	—	—	—	1	1
J. McNamara	—	—	—	—	—	—	—	—	1	1

TOTAL LEAGUE GOALS—868

	'66	'67	'68	'69	'70	'71	'72	'73	'74	Total
B. Lennox	15	13	32	12	14	10	12	10	13	131
W. Wallace	—	14	21	18	16	19	—	—	—	88
J. Johnstone	9	13	5	5	10	8	9	7	3	69
D. Deans	—	—	—	—	—	—	19	22	24	65
H. Hood	—	—	—	5	8	22	11	12	7	65
S. Chalmers	14	23	9	11	2	2	—	—	—	61
K. Dalglish	—	—	—	—	—	—	17	23	18	58
J. McBride	31	18	4	1	—	—	—	—	—	54
J. Hughes	13	6	7	10	10	5	—	—	—	51
T. Gemmell	4	9	4	8	9	1	—	—	—	35
B. Murdoch	5	4	6	4	5	2	4	4	—	34
L. Macari	—	—	—	1	7	5	10	4	—	27
B. Auld	8	7	5	1	5	—	—	—	—	26
B. McNeill	—	—	6	3	5	1	3	—	—	18
T. Callaghan	—	—	—	3	2	2	1	2	2	12
V. Davidson	—	—	—	—	1	5	5	—	—	11
C. Gallagher	4	2	—	—	—	—	1	—	—	7
D. Hay	—	—	—	—	1	—	3	2	—	6
J. Brogan	—	—	1	2	1	—	1	—	—	5
G. Connelly	—	—	—	—	—	1	—	3	1	5
P. McCluskey	—	—	—	—	—	—	—	3	1	4
S. Murray	—	—	—	—	—	—	—	3	—	3
P. McMahon	—	—	1	1	—	—	—	—	—	2
I. Young	2	—	—	—	—	—	—	—	—	2
D. Cattanach	—	—	1	—	—	—	—	—	—	1
J. Craig	1	—	—	—	—	—	—	—	—	1
J. Divers	1	—	—	—	—	—	—	—	—	1
D. McGrain	—	—	—	—	—	—	—	1	—	1
B. McLaughlin	—	—	—	—	—	—	—	1	—	1
J. Quinn	—	—	1	—	—	—	—	—	—	1
Own goals	—	2	3	2	1	3	3	2	1	17

TOTAL 868

teams in the friendly, but to win at any time in England was gratifying and the travelling support revelled in it. They serenaded the manager:

It's magic, you know,
It's got to be ten in a row.

It would remain nine in a row. The run of unbroken success was at an end, although no one knew it. In this unequalled consistency of success, Stein had used 44 players. Fittingly and pleasingly Billy McNeill, a superlative captain, played more often than anyone else. In nine full seasons he missed only 24 matches out of 306. Johnstone and Murdoch each played more than 200 times and one more game would have put Bobby Lennox on the same mark. As it was, in 199 games he scored an astonishing 131 goals. Yet Andy Lynch and Jackie McNamara who each made but one appearance are part of the marvellous fact, part of the legend. That legend had been created by 44 players, three different elevens and one manager.

12

TWILIGHT OF THE GOD

EARLY on a Sunday morning in July 1975 a Mercedes car driven by Jock Stein was in collision with a Peugeot on the notorious A74 road near Lockerbie in Dumfriesshire. There were four other passengers in the car, Jean, his wife, Bob Shankly, who had succeeded Stein with Hibs, Shankly's wife, Margaret and Stein's great friend of long standing, Tony Queen. The party was returning from holidaying in Minorca where they had been staying at Queen's villa. The collision was head-on and the impact fearful. The two women and Bob Shankly were comparatively unharmed but Stein and Queen were gravely injured. They were removed immediately to Dumfries Royal Infirmary where the new building had been opened by Her Majesty Queen Elizabeth II only two days beforehand.

The condition of the two men gave rise to considerable anxiety and if almost all of the press attention was focused on Stein that was simply because he was so much the better known. He underwent an immediate operation to relieve his breathing but although in considerable pain he displayed remarkable courage, even managing to joke with the nurses by means of scribbled notes. For a few days he was in some danger but his positive personality and magnificent physique pulled him through in conjunction with meticulous medical care.

With regard to the crash, he and his companions were absolute victims, the other car having been travelling on the wrong side of a dual carriageway. The A74, the trunk road which connects Glasgow with Carlisle had a dismal reputation as being one of the most dangerous highways in Britain. At the time of the accident there had been 69 deaths on it during the preceding four years and indeed in the previous month there had been a horrifying coach crash in which 10 holiday-makers from Brighton had been killed.

Stein had the reputation of being a fast but essentially cautious driver and it was a road which he knew well, as he was in the habit of going down to the Manchester and Liverpool areas to take in mid-week English matches. The road was a deathtrap. By coincidence the *Glasgow Herald* had been running a campaign to have it upgraded to acceptable main-road standards. The local Member of Parliament, Mr

Hector (later Sir Hector) Monro voiced the misgivings of many when he said, "I believe that central barriers and better accesses could be provided speedily and results might be obtained by monitoring the speeds of commercial vehicles, supposed to be limited to 40 m.p.h." Mr Monro felt sufficiently strongly to table a question for the Secretary of State in which he enquired what action the latter proposed to take to improve safety on the A74. He also desired to know the number of prosecutions against car, lorry and bus drivers for speeding and a comparison of traffic figures for the A74 and the A1. The *Glasgow Herald* asked another, more intriguing question. Was it true that local drivers, relying on local knowledge were in the habit of taking dangerous short-cuts? The inference was inescapable. The dangerous short-cuts included using carriageways for short distances to go in the opposite direction from that intended.

Three years later Stein was to raise an action in the Court of Session against the other driver involved and after a further delay of more than two years he received a very substantial sum of money as an out of court settlement, the other driver having been convicted of reckless driving, fined and disqualified. It was November 1979 before the affair could be finally laid to rest.

It is necessary to give the background to this accident because there is a tendency to assume that a returning holiday-maker, a football manager used to driving against the clock, would have been liable to have been at fault. There was no question of this. A person in Stein's position — he was well described that very week-end by Ian Archer of the *Glasgow Herald* as "arguably the most important man working in this nation at this time" — was always likely to have his actions magnified for good or ill.

Since one of his fellow-passengers was the well-known Glasgow bookmaker Tony Queen this may be the place to comment on Stein's reputation as a gambler. He had all the miner's liking for games of chance and he was certainly an assiduous attender at race meetings but he was nothing like the Gaylord Ravenal of terracing imagination. Part of the attraction of race meetings for him was that they provided one of the very few outlets away from football which relaxed him and he almost certainly valued them because he could for a short time be in the company of men for whom football was not necessarily a major concern. In the folklore of the terracings his testimonial match was known as the Tony Queen benefit, but that does less than justice to the financial acumen of the two men concerned. At the end of his life Stein was quoted as having left £172,000, scarcely the hallmark of a reckless improvident.

None of this engaged the attention of Scotland in those early July days. There was a gradual easing of tension as it became clear that all concerned in the crash were going to survive. Within a week Stein was expressing a desire to see the Open Golf Championship, which was being held at Carnoustie, on television and his son George duly delivered a set. Yet, however he himself sought to make light of things he had been in a very bad car crash and was lucky to have emerged alive, Tony Queen being arguably even luckier. Three weeks later the Scotland team manager, Willie Ormond, would make an unscheduled visit to Dumfries but would not be allowed to see him although by that time Stein was up and about. There would be no question of his being able to play an active part at Parkhead for many months to come. This was confirmed by two of the people closest to him when, after a month in hospital, he was eventually allowed to go home on 1 August. His wife described him as follows: "He is very tired and I don't expect he will be able to speak about his experience for a few days." Desmond White hinted at a longer period on the sidelines: "Jock Stein will return to the club in his own good time, whenever he feels fit and able after whatever period of convalescence he needs."

The challenge of regaining the championship from Rangers and indeed of winning the newly devised Premier League of ten clubs for the first time was perforce entrusted to his assistant manager Sean Fallon. The first weeks of the season were sufficiently cheerful to hasten the manager's recovery. In a pre-season friendly Derby County were beaten 1-0 and such victories over prestigious opposition from England were always welcomed by supporters and treasurer. George Connelly came in from the outback, Dalglish re-signed and one of the best signings of the mid-1970s was accomplished when the Icelandic international Johannes Edvaldsson was persuaded to move from Danish football.

These were but portents of a false dawn. Stein had hoped to make a quick come-back, had indeed attended a reserve game towards the end of August and a first-team match in early September. But he was far from fit and before the season was out would have to visit a hospital in Manchester for a toe operation. The League Cup final was lost to Rangers by a single goal at Hampden. Worse was the collapse at Fir Park in the Scottish Cup against Motherwell which saw a two-goal lead overhauled and the exit given. Just before the Fir Park match, Stein's son, George, had made one of his rare public appearances when he accepted a purse of ten gold sovereigns on his father's behalf to mark ten years' managership of Celtic.

The season slipped away as Celtic, deprived of Stein's leadership, drifted. Uncertainty showed itself when Jimmy Smith was brought up on trial from Newcastle United. A very gifted player, his fitness was in great doubt as he proved unable to establish any claim to a permanent place. From now on the curious signings would begin to outnumber the good, culminating in the astonishing decision to give the captaincy in

1977-78 to Frank Munro, signed from Wolverhampton Wanderers on an impermanent basis when again the fitness of a player was in some doubt. Celtic had led the league comfortably at New Year and then proceeded to throw it away hand over fist. For the first time in the last ten years the trophy cupboard was bare, nor had any impact been made in Europe.

The invalid on his sick bed had no fevered delusions about the strength of the current Celtic challenge in Europe. Writing in the Celtic handbook for season 1975-76, the season in which he would play so little part, he described the previous season's effort in what he always regarded as his favourite competition, and the major one. "We were eliminated in the European Cup in the first round by Olympiakos of Greece, a result in sad contrast with some of our glory seasons. I am afraid the only consolation is that if we were not good enough for the competition it was better to get out the way quickly and let others who were get on with it." Harsh words, but the maestro would be back at his desk for the start of 1976-77 and he would have the help of David McParland, former manager of Partick Thistle, who would henceforth be his assistant.

August 1976 saw Stein back in control at Parkhead and he moved

Playing at the Palace — John Stein C.B.E. and Mrs Stein after the Celtic manager had been invested with the C.B.E. at Buckingham Palace.

swiftly to counteract an early defeat from Rangers in the final of the Glasgow Cup. His response was to make what could fairly be described as his last highly successful signing, Pat Stanton of Hibernian. This signing came like a thunderclap because the name of Stanton was inextricably associated with Hibernian, for whom he had played since 1963. The highly intelligent Alan Gordon of Hibernian, in whom Stein had shown an interest on two previous occasions, went through to Parkhead with Stanton on the day of the transfer and remembers vividly the reception the new Celtic player had from the crowd as he was introduced to them during the interval of a match against Dundee United. Stein had forgotten nothing about showmanship during his time away.

Stein's interest in Gordon went back to the time of the signing of Willie Wallace and he later approached Hibernian about a possible transfer but Eddie Turnbull was reluctant to let the tall fair-haired forward go. Gordon's great strength lay in his ability to hover in the air and knock down headed passes for scavenging forwards. Had the transfer gone through it would have been an interesting variation on Stein's normal style of play since in all the years of success Celtic never had a tall forward who was particularly good in the air.

Hibernian kept Gordon, possibly bearing in mind the old dictum that you can get away with transferring a midfield player, and allowed Stanton to go, a move which was hugely unpopular with the Hibernian support. Given the stage at which Stanton's career found itself, it would have been unrealistic to expect more than three seasons from him and in fact he played in a Celtic jersey for only one year, but his influence was immense and he was a player for whom both Stein and the support had an abiding affection. Literally within days of leaving Parkhead, in almost his last action as a manager of Celtic, Stein took a side through to play at Easter Road in a benefit match for Stanton. On a particularly unpleasant day almost 30,000 supporters, the bulk of them Celtic fans, turned out to pay their tribute to a model professional footballer.

The aftermath of that game is interesting for two revelations of Jock Stein's thoughts on professional football and professional footballers. At the reception which followed, at the King James VI Hotel, he was not pleased by the number of "freeloaders" attending and swarming round the buffet. "You shouldn't need to have anything like this and these people shouldn't be here just because the food is there. The player was worth it as a player, they should keep the expenses down so that the profit goes to him," He was even less pleased by the absence of two Anglo-Scots who had been invited to take part and who had declined. Significantly, when Stein became international manager three months later, the two players had no further role to perform in a Scottish jersey. He was warm in his praise of Alan Rough who had made the effort and turned out in goal: "The boy did himself no harm today." The words do not sound particularly warm but Stein had a long memory for friends and foes.

There were other signings, one hardly less spectacular. To the very end Stein never lost his gift for wrong-footing media and public and there was no greater instance of this than the signing of Alfie Conn from Tottenham Hotspur. Players had come to Celtic from England before, but not when their previous club had been Rangers. Conn came from a good stable — his father had been one of the marvellous Heart of Midlothian inside trio of the 1950s, Conn, Bauld and Wardhaugh, and the son was a talented player with a somewhat light and airy approach to his duties.

Stein thought that Conn could do a job for him and the signing would have the additional benefit, as he saw it, of riling the huge Rangers support. It would also strengthen his contention that Celtic were prepared to play anyone regardless of previous background and Stein himself knew how unlikely it was that such a signing could have happened in reverse. Within three months of arrival Conn had picked up a League and Scottish Cup medals double as had Stanton and the other major signing, Joe Craig from Partick Thistle. It was Craig who scored the flag-winning goal at Easter Road, with a penalty kick, converted by Andy Lynch, being enough to defeat Rangers in the final of the Scottish Cup. It was the sixth time in Stein's 12 years at Parkhead that the double had been achieved.

The supporters naturally saw the season in simple terms. Stein had been away the season before and nothing had been achieved. Stein was now back and all was well. The manager knew that things were not as clear-cut as that. There was the matter of European competition and in that Celtic had been bundled out of the UEFA Cup first time round by Wislaw Krakow, not normally regarded as one of the top Polish sides. It was yet another reminder that in European terms Celtic had ceased to count, and to a man who believed that the main value of the Scottish League Championship was as the key to Europe, this was not a situation which could be accepted gracefully.

There would be time for that. He was back at work, he was working well, the new signings were slotting in as he would have wished and his return to Celtic Park had reimbued the entire playing staff with confidence. The seeds of doubt had been resown at Ibrox and that could only improve Celtic's chances in the immediate future. The most observant student of the Scottish football scene would scarcely have predicted that 12 months on Celtic Football Club would have a new manager. There had been a change at the head of the national side with Willie Ormond moving back to club football with Hearts. Stein as ever had been associated with the vacancy and as ever it had gone elsewhere, to Alistair McLeod of Aberdeen. Stein had often expressed a wish to finish his course with Celtic and this was surely now what he would do.

13

THE PARTING OF THE WAYS
AND A LOOK AT LEEDS

A S the season of 1977-78 drew to an end great changes were on the way both in the history of Celtic Football Club and in the professional career of Jock Stein. A partnership was about to be dissolved which had lasted for 13 years and which had brought the East End club unprecedented success.

The season which was just finishing was however, by any objective standards, a dismal failure. Celtic had won no major trophy. They had finished a wretched fifth in the Premier League which contained only ten clubs and their points tally of 36 for the same number of matches meant that they finished out of sight behind the winners, Rangers, who had amassed 19 points more. In the Scottish Cup there had been a humiliating defeat at the hands of First Division Kilmarnock who had got a fighting draw at Parkhead and then upset accepted wisdom that no one got two chances against the 'Old Firm'. The final of the League Cup had been reached but there too defeat was Celtic's portion and defeat against a not over-distinguished Rangers side at that.

All this might have been put down to the kind of fallow season that even the greatest managers and clubs experience periodically but there were other, more serious, underlying symptoms. Celtic had been convincingly dismissed from the European Cup by SW Innsbruck, a hard-working Austrian side who were by no means numbered with the European élite. The Celtic staff contained players — Munro, Dowie, Fillipi, Kay — who tried commendably but lacked either full fitness or pace or even the simple downright skills which would have established them as long-term prospects. Questions were beginning to be asked about the efficiency of the club's scouting system and its willingness to spend heavily in the transfer market if need be.

The fact that Celtic had slipped out of serious consideration for the major European prizes was reflected in the growing number of players who had left for England over the last five years. The reasons for the departures were complex and it would be inaccurate to portray them as a result of a deliberate policy by the club to cash in on its major assets but the results of those transfers were severely damaging.

With the move to Chelsea of David Hay, following the World Cup

Finals of 1974, Celtic lost an inspirational player and one who could have captained them for many years. Worse, with the waygoing of Hay, George Connelly was almost certainly lost to the game. Connelly had problems of adjustment to the role of international football player which were certainly not of the club's making and he periodically absented himself from training. He had a regard and respect for David Hay and it is arguable that had the latter remained at Parkhead, Connelly might have been able to overcome his anxieties and fill that major role for which he was so uniquely qualified. As it was he drifted dispiritedly down and out of organised football and a great talent was lost to Celtic through sheer misfortune.

The loss of Hay might have been survived for Stein's own dictum was that 'you could always get away with transferring a midfield man'. The loss of such as Lou Macari and Kenny Dalglish was harder to bear and indeed, in the latter case, the damage done was irretrievable. Macari had in fact played comparatively few games for Celtic and he could be demanding, as witness his criticism of the Scottish arrangements in Argentina which led to the caustically worded official observation that perhaps it would be better if the player were not exposed to those arrangements again. But whatever his personal quirks he was in the nippy, lethal tradition of Wallace and McBride and it could be argued that he was never satisfactorily replaced. His transfer to Manchester United had its odd side. Stein was credited with a preference that the player should have gone to Liverpool and the final negotiations with Manchester United and the machinery of transfer were carried out not by him but by assistant manager, Sean Fallon.

Dalglish was simply irreplaceable. The finest club footballer in Britain over the period 1970-85, he combined, most unusually, the differing gifts of a highly individual talent and astonishing durability. Not only his goal-scoring record is staggering, so too is the number of matches in which he has taken part. Star players, particularly forwards, normally come much more fragile. There is no reason to believe that Celtic did not do everything they could to keep the player at Parkhead but his going south was deeply resented by the supporters.

Dalglish had been a notable absentee from the summer tour of Australia where Celtic had played Red Star Belgrade, Arsenal and the Australian national eleven. Doubts had been expressed about the wisdom of undertaking so long a trip which would involve highly competitive matches but the injuries to Stanton and Conn which followed were more attributable to sheer bad luck.

An article in the *Sunday Mail* of 21 August 1978 seemed to hint that Celtic had not pulled out all the stops in their effort to keep Dalglish at Parkhead and a letter in the *Celtic View* of three days before had foreshadowed this: "The problem of losing star players is not exclusive to Scotland or even Great Britain but it signals the end of club loyalty and makes Kenny's platitudes about leaving rather empty."

Desmond White and Stein were both emphatic that there had been no prospect of keeping Dalglish at Parkhead. Just before the final meeting with the Liverpool officials which saw the transfer concluded White had said to the player: "We very much want you to remain with Celtic. Could you in any way be persuaded to stay?" To which Dalglish had replied, "Mr White, it is not a question of money." Two minutes before going into the room where the transfer was to take place Stein had made a final appeal, "Is there anything we can do to make you change your mind?" But the answer was "No."

Both men were equally convinced that Celtic would in any event have got little more from the player. White said that it had got to the stage where Kenny Dalglish was practically incapable of giving his best to the club, and in the same issue of the official newspaper, Stein added his final thoughts: "There was nothing to be gained by hanging on to a player who has lost his enthusiasm for the club and wants to leave. Kenny had shown no desire to turn out for us this year."

Probably Dalglish's own version of events which he gave in an interview with Richard Bott of the Scottish *Sunday Express* in January 1978 is as close to reality as we are likely to get. "I'd no crib with Celtic when I decided I wanted to leave them. I simply left one club for another. It was simply a question of wanting to try something else. Perhaps that is a bit selfish but if you don't try, you don't know."

At such a transitional and disturbing time it would be no more than expected that Stein and Celtic should, additionally, run out of luck. Steve Murray and Pat Stanton, two fine signings who might have done much to restore flagging fortunes (although Stanton in particular was a short-term investment), suffered serious injuries which finished their careers. Even sadder was the injury to Brian McLaughlin right at the outset of his playing days which left him still able to play football but not quite at top level. A genuine and marvellous talent was thereby lost to the game and the club.

All this might have been ridden out but for the questions which inevitably arose about Stein's health and motivation. He had done marvellously well to recover as he had done from the fearful car crash of 1975. Such a recovery would have been beyond all but the strongest of men. Had he been able to recapture his verve, the determination which would be needed to take the side again over the so-familiar road for the championship? After his accident he had been away from day-to-day administration at Parkhead for a year. Could he re-establish himself with the players? Had he done that with the championship of 1976-77 and how important was that set against the fact that Rangers had taken the championship in three out of the last four seasons? Was the pendulum swinging fully back?

The impetus came from Ibrox. On 24 May 1978 Rangers announced that their manager, Jock Wallace, was leaving for unspecified reasons (they remain unspecified) and that the managership would be assumed by one of the most popular players ever to play for them — John Greig. Four days later a corresponding announcement was made from Parkhead that Jock Stein would step down from the position of manager and be replaced by the man he himself had chosen as club captain, Billy McNeill, who would move south from Aberdeen.

The decisions may well have been arrived at totally simultaneously but the timing of them gave the impression that for once in a way Celtic were reacting to an initiative taken by their oldest rivals. McNeill would be a popular choice with the supporters, there was no doubt of that. He had been an extremely successful player. More important, he had seen Parkhead as the hub of his footballing fortunes and he had been a dignified and imposing skipper. According to club chairman Desmond White, writing in the *Celtic View* of August 1978 Stein himself had been involved in the consultative process which would not, only take Billy McNeill from Pittodrie but would see the departure of Sean Fallon, a loyal and long-term servant, together with the much more recently appointed David McParland, the Celtic assistant manager.

At a press conference the chairman had set out the background to the latest turn of events: "It is a truism that no matter how talented and successful a manager the time comes when the pressures and strains start to take their toll. As well as knowing better than most just what those pressures are, Jock Stein suffered severe physical injury as the innocent victim of a major car accident. These factors combined to bring home to him several months ago that the time was opportune for the directors to consider seriously the question of a successor."

It was further announced that a new post would be created for Stein in recognition of his unparalleled services to the club. He would be invited to join the Board and his responsibility would be to help develop the commercial side of things. A remarkable photograph of the time shows chairman Desmond White and the new manager with linked outstretched hands while behind them, as though cut off by a barrier is the brooding, almost bewildered face of the outgoing chief.

The hand-over was an instance of how difficult it is to effect an amicable transfer of power. There was no doubt that the Premier League was going to be harder to win than the old-style First Division had ever been. It was apparent by the late 1970s that there could now be not one but three rivals who would have to be taken very seriously. In addition to Rangers, Aberdeen and Dundee United now aspired to the regular winning of championships and trophies. Perhaps at the age of almost 56 Jock Stein was beginning to find the track-suited part of the job a little overtaxing.

Much was made of the fact that Stein, a non-Catholic, had been appointed to the Board of Directors but there does not seem to have been anymore reason why he should not have been than there was any reason for not making him manager 13 years before. What is certain is that Stein had no sooner accepted the post than he began to have second thoughts.

Celtic were criticised for having offered their ex-manager "a non-job" but such criticism is harsh and misplaced. The commercial side of the game becomes ever more important and provided that the Board of Directors was prepared to give him his head, there was certainly valuable work to be done. It may be that Stein doubted his own capabilities in this area, it was just as likely that he would miss the day-to-day involvement with footballers, given his innate conviction that only the playing of football mattered. He certainly voiced this thought when he eventually decided to take the Leeds United job: "I did not want to stay with Celtic as a director. I felt I had too much to offer football and I wanted a closer involvement."

Herein lay the essence of the conflict. John Fairgrieve, a vigorous writer with a fine cutting edge and a gift for controversy, declared in the *Sunday Mail* of 27 August 1978 that Stein had, in essence, been offered a job as ticket vendor for the Celtic Development Fund. The club was indignant at this suggestion and their viewpoint was that the ex-manager had been offered a working directorship with special responsibility for development projects.

It is especially difficult for the great to go — to make the clean break. To the end of his life Bill Shankly could not come to terms with the reality that it was not appropriate for him to travel in the Liverpool team bus now that he was no longer their manager. In a quote given by Desmond White to the *Glasgow Herald* on 17 August 1978 ther are perhaps signs that the chairman himself was coming round to this opinion: "If Leeds United have made an offer of a large sum of money to Mr Stein then we as a club could hardly stand in his way if he wanted to accept the challenge."

The best outcome might well have been for Celtic to have cut the painter absolutely. The most obvious precedent for retaining a manager as part of the Board was not an immediately promising one. There is little doubt that the presence of Sir Matt Busby in the boardroom at Old Trafford made it difficult, in some instances impossible, for a succession of young managers to settle in with Manchester United. Busby's own fine record and the universal veneration with which he was regarded cast far too long a shadow for his successors. It was hard to resist the impression of the Emperor in exile and indeed on at least one occasion Sir Matt came back to take over in a temporary managerial capacity.

Perhaps Celtic should simply have thanked Stein in the following terms: "We are enormously indebted to you for the astonishing work you have done on behalf of the club. We hope that the salary we have paid you and the facilities we have accorded you for writing and broadcasting have been something approaching an adequate reward and we are pleased that your testimonial match turned out so well. You will be a welcome guest at Parkhead whenever you care to return and if we can ever be of service we will expect you to call on us." There was really no mid-point between making Stein chairman of the club and allowing him to go.

The testimonial game had taken part at Celtic Park on 14 August 1978, with Liverpool supplying the opposition in a match which the visitors won 3-2. Dalglish was on hand to let the Celtic fans see what they were missing. The programme had declared that "there will be a smashing welcome home reception for Kenny when he turns out in the red of Liverpool at Celtic Park tonight" but this prophecy was very wide of the mark. Dalglish's reception ranging from the cool to the downright hostile.

Bill Shankly was always individual in his expression but never more so than in the testimonial game programme: "Aye but of course you know me too, I like to talk. And Jock's worth talking about. A great manager, my pal for years. A great man as well, with a heart of gold who'd give his last shilling. . . . Aye, Stein knows it all. He's the best. And that's me, Billy Shankly once of Liverpool, saying so. I ken you'll agree." What is interesting about that quote is the phrase "I ken you'll agree" which doesn't sound like Shankly at all and the rather wistful echo, "once of Liverpool". Here was another man who had given up full-time managership and come to regard that decision as a hideous mistake.

The match was attended by 60,000 spectators and gate receipts totalled £80,000. The Lord Provost of Glasgow, David Hodge, had acted as Honorary President of the Appeals Committee and the patrons included five prominent parliamentarians, Secretary of State Bruce Millan, Minister of State Gregor McKenzie, Parliamentary Under-Secretaries Hugh Brown and Frank McElhone, with Teddy Taylor from the Conservative Party and the Archbishop of Glasgow, the Most Reverend T. J. Winning. Serving on the Committee were his former business partner Jimmy Gordon of Radio Clyde and his own great friend, prominent Glasgow bookmaker, Tony Queen.

Inevitably, it was an emotional evening and there was little fore-warning that Stein was about to sever a working connection which had lasted for a quarter of a century with one interval of five years. In a sense, his decision to move to Leeds was almost as big a surprise as his two previous ones to stay with Celtic and not to cast in his lot with Manchester United when the opportunity arose in 1970 and again in 1974.

Stein was always keenly interested in English football and although profoundly patriotic, and in no narrow chauvinistic sense either, he did regard managership of the top English clubs as the greatest challenge available. He always insisted that his primary reason for declining the Manchester United job was a family one, that Mrs Stein and their children were unwilling to uproot themselves from Glasgow. He himself may well have thought that given the degree of harassment to which children of 'Old Firm' managers are exposed in the extended village which is the Glasgow football community, there might have been less pressure on them in England. However that may be, he decided against going although the decision was both protracted and public.

It is worth observing that although Stein had travelled the world very extensively in the course of his footballing duties he had never operated away from home for any great length of time and the Llanelly experience had been an unhappy one. Even the experience of National Service which accustomed thousands of young Scots to other ways and other places had been denied him because of his mining background. He was too Scottish to flourish easily once removed from his native soil. He may have thought too of the testimonial coming up.

It was, therefore, something of a surprise when he decided to go for the Leeds United job once the first choice for it, Lawrie McMenemy, decided towards the end of July 1978 that he would remain with Southampton. Leeds United were in many respects a peculiar club with more than the whiff of sulphur about them. For many years a team of no great distinction, one whose natural habitat was the Second Division of the Football League, they had emerged in the late 1960s under Don Revie to become the third force after Manchester United and Liverpool.

They were very successful but disliked. They had neither the flamboyance of style of Manchester United nor the good-humoured exuberance of the Liverpool players and support. Under Revie, Leeds earned the reputation of being cynical, grudging, argumentative. They attracted the adjective professional, in the worst sense of the word. They were capable of playing extremely attractive football but for much of the time seemed almost wilfully to exhibit the darker side of their nature. They could never rid themselves of the feeling that they were Johnny-come-latelys to the ranks of the mighty.

Allegations had been made that Leeds through Revie had exerted improper pressure on various opposition players to influence the results of matches and although the accusations were not legally substantiated the club was tarnished. The doubters had a field day when in December 1978 the FA imposed a 10-year ban on Don Revie for bringing the game into disrepute. It did not matter to them that the ban was in connection with Revie's conduct as the national manager rather than as a club one.

Leeds too was not naturally a football city in the way that the great northern strongholds of Manchester and Liverpool were. The hard core of their support did not number much above 15,000 even in 1978 and there was always the unexpressed belief that the club was living beyond its station just a little.

Of the great side of the 1970s only Paul Madeley was left, and Peter Lorimer who was to leave in a matter of months. There were good players on the books, the English internationals Trevor Cherry and Tony Currie and the Scots brothers Frank and Eddie Gray. The impression remained however of a disturbed club which did not know its mind. Four short years before they had hired the best young manager in England, Brian Clough, and then sacked him within 44 days. The almost-universal belief was that the sacking had been brought about at the instigation of the playing staff.

The question, therefore, was whether Stein, never having worked in England before, never having played with an English team, could revive the fortunes of an ailing and suspect club. There had been close contacts between Celtic and Leeds United of course in the aftermath of the European Cup meetings between the two teams. Friendly matches had been played and Celtic had supplied the opposition for Jackie Charlton's benefit match.

The question remained unanswered given the brevity of Stein's sojourn at Elland Road. He managed, just, to exceed Brian Clough's flying visit and his tenure of office lasted a mere 45 days. For some months, since indeed the disastrous visit to Argentina for the World Cup Finals of 1978, Scottish team manager Ally McLeod's hold on his post had been precarious, or as the average Scottish football supporter pithily expressed it, "his jacket was on a shaky nail."

The nail felt after the European Nations match against Austria in Vienna when a gallant fight-back from 3-0 down to 3-2 was not enough to keep the likeable, hyperbolic McLeod in his job.

In the eyes of the press and public there was only one possible successor and that was Stein. He had been reported as having signed a three-year contract with Leeds for a total fee of £85,000 with various additional incentive payments but it turned out that he was not contracted and that the way was open for him to take the Scotland job if it were offered to him. The SFA met on 2 October and made their decision after a protracted seven-hour meeting. They did not make their choice public until two days later and it was therefore 4 October 1978 before Stein officially became manager of Scotland for the second time in his career.

There remained the severance with Leeds. The English club must have been disappointed but said all the right things. In his spell there Stein had taken charge of the club in just seven league games of which three had been won and three lost. When he returned north they were 13th in the league table and by the end of the season had hoisted themselves up to fifth.

Stein's reason for taking the Scotland job was oblique and, in the last analysis, unconvincing. "Money didn't come into it but my family did not want to stay in the Leeds area." Given the previous reservations over the Manchester job it passes belief that the question would not have been thoroughly discussed before he came to the decision to accept the Leeds offer. His children, Rae and George, were young adults by this time and quite capable of sustaining an independent existence. The reasons which had led him to decline the offer of a £60,000 per year job in Kuwait were less telling when applied to the West Riding of Yorkshire.

The players were sorry to see him go and leading scorer Paul Hart spoke for them: "It will throw the club into trauma again. We are playing well as a team and things are picking up under Mr Stein."

The chairman, Manny Cussins, was more emotional although it could well be argued that he was merely perishing on the sword which a few years ago he had presented to Brian Clough: "I am heart-broken. I suggested that Mrs Stein might keep the house in Glasgow for six months or so until we found them a home in Yorkshire but I think that would have been unacceptable. Nothing in my lifetime has worried me more than this, not even the Brian Clough affair."

And what were Stein's final thoughts on the matter of leaving Leeds to take up the national post on his 56th birthday? "The fact that this happened after 44 days was just one of those things. It would have been worse had it happened in the middle of the season but it is terrible for Mr Cussins and the supporters. The Board have done everything possible for me and it was a pleasure to be among them. They wanted me to stay and I am sure I would have been successful. I feel I have let people down and so I am leaving Leeds immediately."

Clearly the big Scot felt more than a little guilty about his hasty departure which would have been more palatable at the Yorkshire end had he said something along the lines of "the running of the national side is the greatest honour which can be bestowed on a Scottish manager". An instance of this unease is the total omission of the episode from his entry in *Who's Who*.

Embarrassed or not, he was now the national manager and his over-riding task would be to bring a sense of reality and reasonable expectation to perhaps the most romantic and emotional body of supporters in the entire world.

14

INTERNATIONAL MANAGER — SECOND TIME ROUND

THE Jock Stein who operated as manager of Scotland was not the same man who performed at club level. The difference was not so much in selection as in style. Both at club and international level Stein exhibited the tendency to make frequent changes, to freshen the team and eliminate complacency, and to go for experience. This had been a hall-mark of his Celtic days, when the Dalglishs, McGrains, Aitkens and Burns's of the world had been greatly outnumbered by the ready-made imports and even those above-named players had served a fairly lengthy apprenticeship.

Stein was a much more cautious manager with the international side and rarely was there evidence of the marvellous freewheeling football which had been the trademark of the Celtic teams of the late 1960s. There were two reasons for this. The first was that he himself had seen how Celtic had become steadily less effective in Europe, to the point where they could scarcely be counted as a European force, as the leading Continental sides worked out for themselves that dash and verve on their own were likely to achieve little unless a team had the marvellous individual talent of a Bobby Murdoch or a Jimmy Johnstone.

The other reason was the volatility of the Scottish support. Stein remembered with distaste the hyperbole of the World Cup campaign of 1978 when a side which had demonstrated that it was incapable of beating any of the home countries in Glasgow was nonetheless given a hysterical send-off a few days later. Scores of thousands of supporters turned up at Hampden Park to witness nothing more exhilarating than an open-topped bus being driven round the track with players waving inanely from it.

In the weeks that followed Stein had watched grimly as the exercise fell apart in a flurry of indiscipline and back-biting. Disaster followed disaster. There was the less than total commitment of the courtesy Scots, Don Masson and Bruce Rioch, there was the embarrassing post-match admission by Willie Johnston that he had taken a prohibited substance, although for medicinal reasons. On the field of play Scotland's refusal to take Peru seriously was justly punished with a 3-1 thrashing and in order to scramble a 1-1 draw with Iran it was necessary

136

Stein at Parkhead — A photograph taken towards the end of the marvellous run of nine league titles in a row.

for one of the Iranian defenders to put the ball through his own goal as no Scottish player was ever likely to score. Even a fine win against Holland in the last match could not redeem a shoddy overall performance.

As a man whose patriotism was never in question Stein took this fiasco to heart, the more so that the venue for it was Argentina, a country which had been branded on his mind since 1967. He came to the job with certain convictions deeply implanted. The first was that all international results must be subordinated to performances in the World Cup. No amount of three-goal victories against Wales or Ireland, which in any event had not been forthcoming, would compensate for poor performances on the greatest of international stages. "Judge me on the World Cup" would be his motto as manager of Scotland.

He understood and partially sympathised with the romantic streak which was shot through the Scottish players and support but equally he knew that it had to be ruthlessly suppressed. It was his task to get the national side playing with the head rather than the heart. In this he knew he would meet opposition: there was a legitimate school of thought which argued that Scots were temperamentally unsuited to a waiting game and should be given their head. No matter, he was determined on a change of style. He also distrusted the influence of the Anglos and their not always unspoken assumption that anyone who could really play this game would be doing it in the Football League. This was not a notion calculated to appeal to someone who had spent his own playing and managerial career in Scotland, and he was also acutely aware that the influence of the Anglo-Scots had often been crucial in luring south players who hitherto had seemed perfectly content with their lot in Scotland. He was far too astute to deprive himself of the services of talented players simply because they happened to play their football in England but there is evidence of a move over the years to the home Scot. Other considerations apart, Stein thought it important that the man who supported the Scottish game week in week out should have the chance of seeing current Scottish international players in abundance in Premier League matches.

He was not the first Scotland manager without experience of international football as a player — neither John Prentice nor Malcolm McDonald had been capped for Scotland — but his appointment in that regard did run contrary to the modern trend. His managerial career was such as to make him impregnable to questioning from the players and there is no doubt that he was the overwhelmingly popular choice for the post. Supporters, seeing the massive solidity of the great figure, were instinctively reassured. They might be beaten, but they were unlikely to be shown up.

The second phase of Stein's career as manager of Scotland began unspectacularly with a European Nations match against Norway at Hampden on 25 October 1978. Scotland had already played one match in this tournament and lost 3-2 to Austria in Vienna. It was a competition in which Scotland had never made the least impact and although Stein started off with a win, as he had made a habit of doing wherever he went, it was a most unconvincing victory. The unregarded Norwegians dominated the match for much of the game and it took a highly debatable penalty — a real home-town decision, in the excellent American phrase — to permit the Scots to scrape through by 3-2.

The Middlesbrough goalkeeper, Jim Stewart, felt the weight of Stein's displeasure and also missing from the next match against Portugal in Lisbon were Graeme Souness, Andy Gray and Arthur Graham. The Scots conformed to pattern by losing 1-0 and making qualification from their group extremely doubtful. Under previous managers Scotland had a very useful record at Hampden where a devoted support and frequently spineless refereeing worked wonders but the international side achieved little when it travelled.

Before the next match in the European Nations competition there was a break for the Home International Championship, a tournament on which the English FA in particular was looking with an even more jaundiced eye. Scotland did not fare particularly well, being thoroughly beaten 3-0 in Cardiff where John Toshack had a hat-trick. Again the goalkeeper, Alan Rough, fell victim to the doctrine of personal responsibility and into the side came George Wood of Everton. His international debut was in a match of numbing tedium against Northern Ireland at Hampden where only the result, a 1-0 win could be regarded as remotely satisfactory.

On the following Saturday at Wembley George Wood added his name to that list of Scottish keepers who have found the big occasion too much for them — Freddy Martin of Aberdeen, Frank Haffey of Celtic and Stuart Kennedy of Rangers. The match was going well, with Scotland in the lead through a John Wark goal, when just before half-time the players were joined by a cretinous figure in bizarre tartan trappings. The police were quick to remove him and the Scotland manager was even quicker but the interruption had been fatal, the Scottish team's concentration disturbed. England equalised just before half-time through a goal which Wood might well have saved and he was again at fault in the second half. England's third goal was beautifully worked and almost certainly unnecessary.

Defeat at the hands of England is never easy to accept but there had been extenuating circumstances. If that fool had not run on to the playing pitch . . . if George Wood had not let nerves get the better of him . . . Jock knew what he was doing . . ..

This conviction was strengthened when in June 1979 Scotland went to Oslo and swept aside those very Norwegians who had caused them such trouble at Hampden. In winning 4-0 the Scots gave one of their best post-war performances away from home and kept themselves in with a chance of qualifying from their section for the final stages. Stein could take a short holiday thinking that it was coming right.

The preparation for the Norwegian game had been a match against the 1978 World Cup winners, Argentina, at Hampden Park. The game was noteworthy for the appearance amongst the established South American stars, Tarantini, Passarella, Houseman, Luque, of the infant phonomenon Diego Maradona. The Scots performed well enough but Argentina, in winning 3-1 on a tight rein, provided what Stein had been hoping his players would get — a vivid illustration of the gap that exists between artist and artisan. The lesson was not meant to daunt but to inspire and to encourage the home side to emulate. In September 1979 the Peruvians were forgiven for their effrontery in Argentina and invited to Hampden but revenge was not forthcoming and the Scots had to be content with a 1-1 draw.

With the autumn the pursuit of the European Nations Cup was resumed but a goalkeeping blunder by Alan Rough gave Austria a rather fortunate 1-1 draw at Hampden Park on a wet night when 72,700 people turned out to watch. Two losses against Belgium, 2-0 in Brussels and a humbling 3-1 thrashing at Hampden Park, extinguished Scottish interest in the competition and as proof that the patience of the Scottish footballing public was not inexhaustible, the attendance for the return Belgian game in Glasgow was a miserable 25,000. The final dead match of the competition against Portugal produced a meaningless 4-1 victory and Scotland finished in fourth place of a five-nation section.

So far, then, the new manager had scarcely delivered the goods at international level and anxiety grew with the approaching World Cup competition of 1980-1982 on which Stein had staked his reputation and, to some extent, his credibility. It was not so much that the match record under Stein was bad — although it was — as the fact that after almost a year of his leadership no discernible playing system could be seen to have emerged, making all allowances for injuries and unavailability of England-based players.

As a result of an FIFA decision to increase the number of finalists in Spain in 1982 from 16 to 24, two countries would qualify from the section of five in which Scotland found itself. The rivals for those Spanish places would be Sweden, Northern Ireland, Portugal and Israel with accepted wisdom having it that Sweden and Portugal would be the main threats. It was not the most taxing of sections but always in the background was the spectre of Scotland's abysmal away record.

The team which went to Stockholm in September 1980 to begin the qualifying stages had no great previous form behind it. A defeat by

England at Hampden had been followed by two others at the hands of Poland and Hungary during a summer tour. Stein had now managed five wins in 18 starts and there had been 11 losses. Among some reporters and even from some quarters of the support, the murmurings were beginning that perhaps the big man was past it at top level.

The preparations for the match were dogged by the familiar chain of injuries with Kenny Burns, David Narey and Graeme Souness all having to pull out. Stein took comfort from the fact that Sweden had already played and had had a bad result, dropping an unexpected home point to Israel. The Scots manager saw this as a distinct bonus: "Although Israel will cause problems here and there they won't be in the top two at the finish. If we beat the Swedes I feel it'll reduce the odds to any two from three [Scotland, Northern Ireland, Portugal]." As always he was anxious to damp down overexuberance: "I have stressed to them [the players] that a simple shot into the net gains the same reward as a spectacular goal. Our strikers seem to have some sort of obsession with scoring 'great' goals and this is a fault they must iron out. . . . In the past several players were inclined to play only for themselves and this will not be tolerated. . . . If we play only half as well as the Swedes think we can then we should get the result we came for."

The Scots in winning 1-0 returned one of their better European performances of recent years and the goal which secured victory was a brilliantly worked affair between Gordon Strachan and Archie Gemmill with the former finishing off the move. The win was doubly valuable for having been recorded away from home and the Scots showed commendable composure in defending their narrow lead over the last few minutes.

Scotland and Stein were well prepared to meet the Portuguese in the second qualifying game at Hampden Park on 15 October 1980. Only Alex McLeish was unavailable and Stein felt that the victory in Stockholm had bought time for Scotland: "After winning the first game we can afford to be patient against the Portuguese. Otherwise we would have been forced to chase things right from the start and that can be fatal."

He was anxious as ever that the pre-match thinking should be positive and he was at pains to stress that he had a powerful squad at his disposition. There was a hint of the anger he felt at the occasional Scottish tendency to depreciate their own players: "Our own players are often respected more by others than by their own countrymen." He would, unlike his club days, be prepared to sacrifice style for content: "Not many bouquets go to good-playing losers. Sweden, who play in Belfast tomorrow, have already got off to a poor start and if we can ensure that Portugal have a similar beginning to their campaign then that will put two of the strongest sides in the group under pressure." He had an oblique warning for the Scottish support: "I think our fans know now that you can't come out and run all over the opposition in games like this. Our support is better than ever before. We've the most experienced side of all the home countries as regards World Cups and therefore the most experienced fans."

At Hampden on the night of 15 October, the most experienced fans in Great Britain booed their side heartily as they were held to a lack-lustre goalless draw. Stein, however was not in the market for being unduly depressed by the failure to win or even score: "If we'd played badly then I'd have needed to ask questions, but we didn't and I'm prepared to stand by these players. . . . When you look at the situation we're pretty well off. When the qualifying draw was made I think everyone would agree that the two toughest sides in the group were Sweden and Portugal. We've played them both, we've three points and if we take three points from every two games we'll qualify for Spain in 1982. . . . They played totally defensively. You could set out eleven dust bins in the penalty area and that would cause problems. The most pleasing aspect for me on Wednesday was that we didn't lose our heads. The normal Scottish attitude when things are not going well is to go for win or bust. That can be dangerous for then you lose your discipline and leave yourself open."

The national manager was entitled to be pleased with the return from the first two games and there was then a break for four months before the meeting with the unrated Israel in Tel Aviv. The Scottish party left a snow-covered Glasgow with only Alan Brazil unavailable for selection. In the reverse of the show-business cliché, an excellent rehearsal was the prelude to a dismal performance. Stein had been delighted with the attitude of the players in training: "They were all out to impress today and that's the way to approach such a match. The strikers in particular worked so hard that on today's performance you would have wanted all three to play. . . . The team I've chosen is not necessarily the one I'd have chosen against more fashionable opposition."

Someone had omitted to inform the Israelis that they were unfashionable and the Scots 1-0 victory was almost attributable to a performance of sustained brilliance from Alan Rough in the Scottish goal and a pivoting flash of genius from Kenny Dalglish. Stein was both furious and relieved: "The first half was a complete shambles because Israel got to the ball first on every occasion. Rough, fortunately for us, was brilliant." Next day, he was happier on reflection: "I'd settle for Wednesday's result in the next three matches at home against Northern Ireland, Israel and Sweden. That would give us eleven points and a qualifying place. After that we can think about putting on the good suits."

A month later, in the first of the three home matches, with Northern

Ireland as opponents, he did not get as good a result. Dalglish had to drop out through injury after a record 43 consecutive appearances in a Scottish international jersey and Graeme Souness was also missing. The manager was quite curt in discussing these losses: "The game is all about those players who are available." The truth of this is indisputable but it explains the overwhelming anxiety of the professional footballer who suspects with good reason that to be out of the first team is to become a non-person.

The two players were certainly missed. The Irish held out against everything the Scots could send against them and then went ahead with a Hamilton header with just 20 minutes left. John Wark managed an equaliser within a few minutes before the 79,000 crowd could really turn against the home team but there was neither time nor the skill to provide a winner. Scotland were unbeaten after four outings but had failed to win on either occasion at Hampden Park, as Stein remarked with a certain amount of discontent. He pointed out that Scotland with a reputation as a poor away side had nevertheless two away wins as against two home draws. "We never seem to make it easy for ourselves in the World Cup."

A month later Israel visited Hampden for the return match. One flurry disturbed the usual World Cup routine of Sunday check of injuries, Monday assessing availability, Tuesday prediction of outcome, Wednesday playing of actual match and Thursday post-mortem. Andy Gray was reclaimed by Wolverhampton Wanderers, who maintained that he had a slight hamstring injury. Stein was annoyed that he found out about this from the newspapers but managed to grit that if the player's manager, John Barnwell, said that the lad was unfit then that was it.

He made five changes from the Northern Ireland game, bringing in Souness, Hanson, Provan, Jordan and Hartford while amongst the omitted players was the captain, Archie Gemmill. Stein had picked an all-out attacking side which he described as on paper at least the most adventurous side he had chosen since taking over as Scotland manager. Boldness was rewarded with a 3-1 victory although Israel caused several early problems and were unlucky that the referee thought that a tackle by Danny McGrain on Tabak was within the laws. He did not so interpret two Israeli tackles and the ensuing penalties were both converted by John Robertson with David Provan of Celtic scoring the third. Israel got a late goal but it did not affect the result.

Stein did not thank anybody who pointed out that if the Scots occasionally got the rough edge of fortune abroad, refereeing at Hampden was often scandalously weak and to the home side's advantage. Penalty kicks awarded to visiting sides had a considerable scarcity value whereas over the years the number of penalties contrived by various Scots was quite high. The gravelly voice growled out his post-match summary: "This was Joe Jordan's best-ever performance in a Scottish jersey and the game was made for John Robertson. We have eight points from five matches and are in a good position. Who is to say that we may not do even better away from home? The others are chasing us now."

There was considerable optimism before the last of the three consecutive home games. Stein was in ebullient mood: "The game couldn't have come at a better time for us. At the start of the domestic season the players are fresh and they're also sharp having got a few matches under their belts with their clubs." He told Jim Reynolds of the *Glasgow Herald*: "All through my career as manager I have preferred to play against sides with something to play for. That way, you are always on your toes. Certainly the Swedes are on a good run recently, having won their last four matches without conceding a goal. . . . We'll be going into the match with a sense of urgency and treating it like a typical cup-tie."

Scotland won 2-0 and both goals owed much to the sub-standard performance of the Swiss referee, André Daina. For the first Jordan scored one of his infrequent goals with a fine header from a charitably awarded free kick and there were many who thought that Andy Gray had taken a dive in the tackle which led to the award of a penalty kick and with John Robertson around that meant an automatic goal. Among those who subscribed to the dive theory was Andy Gray himself who in a subsequent television interview admitted that he had cozened the gullible official.

Stein was furious. "We don't want that sort of comment from any of our players. Anyway, Andy was wrong, he was tripped and it was a definite penalty. He shouldn't make comments like that about any referee because what will other referees think in future matches?" What indeed? Stein's anger was not because he thought it had been a penalty kick. It was because Gray's ability to contrive such awards in the future was now severely limited and, worse, some perfectly legitimate claims by him in the future would doubtless be disregarded. Coincidence or not, Gray was not among the names listed in the squad for the next international match which was against Northern Ireland in Belfast on 4 October 1981.

This time the injuries came thick and fast. On the first trawl McGrain, Narey, Provan and Jordan declared themselves unfit and although Davie Cooper of Rangers was co-opted he too had to withdraw and the picture became even murkier when Alex McLeish proved to have been over-optimistic in his assessment of his own fitness. Stein made the best of it — as he later said, he had to make the right kind of noises for the players' benefit. It was almost as though the mass withdrawals in his eyes constituted some kind of arcane advantage: "We'll travel to Belfast with positive thoughts. A point would see us through but we aim to take two. . . . If we qualify for Spain I won't be creating any miracle. After all, two recent managers have taken Scotland to the World Cup finals."

To the normal pressures of a World Cup match were added those imposed by the security situation in Belfast. The Scots were literally in and out visitors and had the worst of a goalless draw, defending desperately and being indebted to Alan Rough in the last few minutes as well as to sundry defenders who hacked the ball desperately from their own goal line. No matter, the point was gained, the section won as it happened and the return game in Lisbon, which it had always been Stein's hope would be a dead game, turned out to be exactly that. He made all the conventional noises about its being important but nobody believed him and perhaps he scarcely expected them to believe him. A Scottish side went there, played reasonably well and lost 2-1. Nobody cared: it was the other section of the Iberian Peninsula that mattered and Scotland would be going there in the summer of 1982.

Before they went, Stein had fallen foul of the Scottish football public as he had never done before. The Home International series of 1982 was not a good one for Scotland. Feeble displays against Northern Ireland and Wales were followed by a 1-0 defeat by England at Hampden and this was the match which aroused great anger among the paying spectators. In the face of an inept Scottish display, the fans were furious at his refusal to bring on Gordon Strachan as the obvious substitution. They had little chance of swaying the manager. Throughout his career Stein almost over-reacted to the notion that anyone might influence his thinking, but his reasons for not doing so after the match were interesting to say the least: "I was not tempted to bring Gordon Strachan on for he had his highlight of the season in the Scottish Cup final last week. It was more important that we keep Gordon fresh for the World Cup in two weeks. Where would we be if he had played against England and been shattered? This is one time we put the World Cup before the England match."

The trouble was that many felt that he had also put the World Cup before the paying customers. They were uneasy too at the statement that a Cup Final, rather than an international against England, should be the highlight of any Scottish player's year. Nor did they like the notion of playing five men at the back in a match against their keenest rivals on home territory. It was perfectly valid for the manager to treat the England game as a semi-competitive practice match for Spain if that was how he saw the absolute overall strategy. What was not acceptable was to charge fancy prices for such a match and give it a Home International championship tag. There was no doubt that Stein had seriously misjudged the temper of the Scottish football supporter and it would take a better than ordinary performance in Spain to remove the sense of disenchantment.

15

THE PENINSULAR CAMPAIGN

THE Scots came to Malaga by way of Portugal and their camp at Sotogrande near Gibraltar. The supporters were vociferous, good-humoured and, a hopeful sign, slightly self-mocking. This was to remove one burden from Stein's shoulders . . . "when there is trouble on the terracings it gets to our players and they can become physical and such". A more durable worry was that the first match would be against New Zealand. He, Stein, had formed the opinion as far back as 1974 in Germany that the so-called underdogs, the completely disregarded entrants for the World Cup, had one good game in them and it was very likely to be on their first appearance. He vividly remembered that failure to take Zaire seriously had cost Scotland a place then, and no one could forget Iran in Argentina, even if that performance, in the Iranians' second game, slightly dented his own theory.

There was a cautionary note sounded in a preliminary radio interview which he gave to Radio Clyde. "We are not going to have a cavalry charge at the New Zealanders by any way. We'll want to settle down. We are hoping though that Strachan and Robertson will play their normal game of attacking people, taking people out of the game, pulling another man out of defence, getting in enough crosses for Brazil and Dalglish with John Wark following in." He explained why he would not name his substitutes until very late on the day. "When you name the 16, it gives the other six a loss and a hole in their day that it's hard for them to fill in. They may be rooming with someone who is playing; they might upset his rest during the day. The fact that you leave naming the other five to the last minute keeps them all on edge and everybody hopes they might be one of the five."

The Scottish side which took the field at the Rosaleda Stadium in Malaga for the first game of the 1982 World Cup Finals lined up as follows: Rough (Partick Thistle); McGrain (Celtic), Gray (Leeds), Souness, Hansen (both Liverpool), Evans (Aston Villa), Strachan (Aberdeen), Dalglish (Liverpool), Brazil, Wark (both Ipswich Town), Robertson (Nottingham Forest).

The Scots demonstrated that they had not lost their ability to roller-coaster between triumph and disaster. They were three goals up at half-time and only the margin of victory seemed in doubt. Then, 20 minutes into the second-half, slack marking allowed the New Zealanders to add a second goal to the one they had already been gifted by a misjudged McGrain pass-back and the game was all set to blow up in Scottish faces yet again. The team drew a collective deep breath, Robertson and Archibald added two more goals to that of Dalglish and the double from Wark before the turn round. Five goals to two and how to see it? A convincing win, a commendable keeping of the head? Or was it another Zaire, a win bought at far too heavy a cost?

The manager seemed, curiously, to be more upset, almost, by the first-half performance. "It could have been much better at half-time. In the second-half we lost our way a wee bit but we came back well in the second part of the half. All in all, being the first game you'd be reasonably satisfied but the team was picked for one game and there will be changes for the next. They didn't come back so much as we let them come back with defensive errors we should have sorted out ourselves." He deflected tersely any efforts to talk at that stage about the forthcoming match against Brazil. "Let's enjoy the night first of all." There had to be hope now that New Zealand could reproduce their second-half form against Russia or Brazil.

For the match against Brazil three nights later, the action moved to Seville. Stein was as good as his word and made four changes, not all as punishment for poor performance although Alan Evans paid the price for being posted missing at the second New Zealand goal. For this match he stood down along with Danny McGrain, Kenny Dalglish and Alan Brazil. Almost twice as big a crowd as had attended the New Zealand match roared this Scottish side on the park: Rough (Partick Thistle); Narey (Dundee United), Gray (Leeds), Souness, Hansen (both Liverpool), Miller, Strachan (both Aberdeen), Hartford (Manchester City), Archibald (Tottenham Hotspur), Wark (Ipswich), Robertson (Nottingham Forest).

After 20 minutes Scotsmen in the Benito Villamarin stadium in Seville looked at each other as though they were seeing visions. Against the best midfield in the world, their side led by a spectacular David Narey goal which if TV commentator Jimmy Hill described it accurately on BBC television must have been the hardest recorded toe-poke in football history. Moreover, the Brazilian defence, not notably world-class, was showing signs of embarrassment as the jubilant Scots swarmed forward.

Zico equalised shortly before half-time with a free kick which would have been beyond the skill of almost any other player in the world but the sides went in level and in the last few minutes the Scots had mounted two promising attacks. On the resumption, however, the airless heat of the Andalusian night and the superior technical skill of the South

Americans began to exact their toll. Oscar scored a bad goal — from the defence's point of view — from a corner kick. Eder added a third with a magnificent chip on the run. In the dying minutes Falcao underlined the difference between honest tradesmen and master craftsmen when he scored a highly individual fourth goal.

Yet the Scots had not been disgraced although the final margin of defeat was emphatic. Stein was not disposed to criticise but rather to pay unfeigned tribute to the class of his opponents. "The players were very satisfied with the first-half; a wee bit disappointed with the first two goals. Some of the players felt they could have been averted. But they're great players and their finishing was clinical and to be beaten by what I think'll be the world champions after giving them such a great first half . . . it left a wee bit of joy with us anyway."

Legitimate pride in performance, even in defeat, would not take Scotland to the next stage of the World Cup finals. Russia had managed to hold Brazil to a single goal, had beaten New Zealand 3-0 and had the comforting knowledge that a draw against Scotland would be good enough. Stein's first task was to rally spirits and convey the impression that psychologically a Scottish team was better geared to going for an outright win rather than playing for the draw. Whether even he believed this must be conjectural, but ability to convince players of even the most improbable happenings had always been his forte. He took what comfort he could from the situation: "They'll not be able to come back like the Brazilians did. The weather didn't suit them either in the Brazil game. If we could get something early on then I don't think they could come back like the Brazilians did. We're looking forward to the game because we've had the extra day off. It will have been a great campaign if we were to qualify for the final stages and everyone behaved themselves."

The Russians would almost certainly behave themselves for since their decision to participate in world football they have almost invariably produced sporting and well-disciplined sides. The Scottish side was that of Seville but with one change in personnel, Jordan coming in for Hartford, thereby committing Scotland to playing a largely aerial game. In the quirky way that football has it was this very same Jordan, often criticised for lack of ball control, who was put clean through after 15 minutes and with an aplomb which no Brazilian could have surpassed calmly placed the ball beyond the Russian keeper, Dasaev. The Scots were ahead. Had the manager got it right or could the Russians come back? There was little sign of it at first and by half-time the Russians only remained in the game courtesy of Dasaev who was reckoned with much justification to be the best goalkeeper in the whole competition.

Even when the teams re-emerged the Russian goal was under a barrage and luck played as much a part as skill in preventing a further downfall. Then an error of judgement by Alan Rough allowed the Russians a soft equaliser, Chivadze scoring with a curiously half-hit shot. Stein now had to gamble and the exhausted Strachan was removed from the scene, as was Jordan. On came McGrain, a great creator but lacking a shot, and Brazil, but almost before they had adjusted Scotland were behind to a goal which made a mockery of any tactical planning.

Hansen and Miller ignored Noel Coward's advice about acting — "Speak clearly and don't bump into people". They failed to speak at all and as a result bumped into each other. The ball broke loose to an astonished Shengelia but although he had fully 40 yards to run in on goal, there was never any doubt of what he would do. Russia were ahead and Scotland were out. In the very last minutes, still going forward, they got back on terms when Souness scored adroitly but this merely meant that for the third World Cup in a row Scotland had been eliminated on goal difference.

Stein was almost bereft of speech. In response to the question "How do you feel?", a question fraught with peril in the circumstances, the manager replied, "I don't know. It's unbelievable. We were punished for any mistakes we made. The boys were . . . we were proud of them all, we should be, they did us proud. We had a glaring penalty kick. I'm 100% sure of that."

This certainty was not shared by SFA Secretary Ernie Walker who was at pains to state that there would be no complaints from the Scots and that in his judgement the referee had handled the game well. He also took great personal pleasure in being able with perfect truth to praise the behaviour of the Scottish fans whose behaviour had been uniformly excellent.

"Judge me by what I do in the World Cup." That had been the constant appeal of the manager. He and his country had done well and had looked in their proper sphere of competition against Russia and even for much of the game against Brazil. At almost 60 years of age time was running out for Stein but he had certainly earned the chance of another tilt at the World Cup — a footballing "last hurrah".

16

MEXICAN PRELIMINARIES

THERE had been some debate about the fitness of Stein to take the Scottish side through the World Cup preliminaries of 1984-86. Yet again the national side had made no impact in the European Nations competition and while the opposition had been respectable — East Germany, Switzerland and Belgium — it could hardly have been described as more than that. The dilemma was a familiar one in politics — to stick with the charismatic but ageing leader, about whom questions were beginning to be asked, or to go for the new and untried?

The World Cup competition grew more complicated with each playing of it, and there were signs of the global malaise in football when the host nation, Colombia, declined the privilege of staging the finals which, after hurried consultation were re-located to Mexico. As in response to a cue the usual quota of rubbish concerning the effects of altitude and heat exhaustion gushed from various British sporting pens in no way deterred by the fact that several European nations had played vigorously there in 1970, as the more successful ones would do again in 1986.

The Scots section, group seven, looked fairly promising with, this time, only four sides — Scotland, Spain, Wales and Iceland. There was a drawback to the smaller section in that only the winners would go forward automatically to the finals with the side in second place having to play off home and away with the winners of the Oceania group, although such a task seemed to involve a long tedious trip rather than particularly formidable on-field opposition.

Stein's assessment of the section was as might have been expected. Spain were the best team in the section and Scotland would do very well to take two points from the matches against them. The two matches against Iceland should furnish maximum points since although several Icelandic players now took part in the major European leagues, the consequences of being unable to defeat a country whose population did not number half a million were unthinkable.

Wales were the jokers in the pack. In Ian Rush and Mark Hughes they had two of the best strikers in Europe and they had a burning incentive to do well. England had, at long last, managed to do away with

151

the Home International Championship on which both the Irish and Welsh FAs had relied for much of their income. Although England had been the prime movers, it was well known that the change had the tacit approval of the SFA and therefore, by extension, of Stein. He had throughout his career been something of a rationaliser of competitions and although for instance he would occasionally defend the Glasgow Cup as providing revenue for such as Clyde, Partick Thistle and Queen's Park, he came increasingly to think that such tournaments were anachronisms and his valuation of them was contained not so much in what he said about them as in the teams he fielded in them. Wales then were annoyed and determined to make their response where it would be most effective, in the prevention of Scotland from qualifying.

In an oddly arranged fixture list, Scotland would play their first two matches at home against Iceland and Spain and follow those with the return game in Spain. To lose either of the Hampden matches would immediately put the national side under severe pressure.

Of the side which took the field against Iceland on 15 October 1984 only Souness, McLeish, Miller and Dalglish had previous World Cup experience. The Scots were already in the debt of the Icelandic team which had astonishingly beaten Wales 1-0 in Reykjavik and in doing so greatly improved Scotland's chances while underlining that they themselves could not be regarded as negligible.

It was an interesting Scottish team that Stein had chosen. He judged that the return of Jock Wallace to manage Rangers had sufficiently galvanised the brilliant but often uninvolved Davie Cooper. The new Celt, Maurice Johnston, signed a few days beforehand from Watford was in the side and so too was Paul McStay. In his pre-match remarks about McStay Stein demonstrated yet again his prophetic gifts: "He has just a wee barrier to go through to be a really great player at this level, but just think what is still to come from him. He just lacks a bit of cheek. If only we could take some from Charlie [Nicholas] and give it to Paul."

McStay, cleverly prompted by the cunning Dalglish who seemed not a whit affected at being dropped from the Liverpool side the previous week, found enough cheek to score two fine goals in a 3-0 win which did not rely on any peculiar refereeing decisions. Nicholas who took over from Dalglish in the later stages had the third goal, so that to a satisfactory all-round performance, Stein could add the bonus of having made a successful substitution. The Iceland side were game and up to a point, clever, but Spain would provide a much more thorough examination of Scotland's prospects of reaching Mexico.

There were no call-offs before the 14 November match against Spain at Hampden, perhaps an indication of how much the players wanted to play. Stein, well aware of the ability of the Spaniards to thwart by clever defensive play, legal and illegal, had the squad work hard at set-pieces in training, to the extent that the famous Italian dummy wall of wooden figures was called into use.

The game proceeded against expectations. First of all, the Spaniards were not noticeably defensive and put the Scottish rearguard under considerable pressure early on. The home side, giving their most exhilarating display in years went two ahead when Maurice Johnston scored twice within nine minutes, his first goal a gem of quick reaction. The Spaniards were forced into defence, not their normal calculating containment but hurried, desperate clearances while Dalglish pulled the puppet strings.

It would not have been a Scotland side had they not contrived to win the hard way. Midway through the second half the Spanish central defender Goicoechia, whose tackling could literally be described as ferocious, got in an off-balance header which should not have beaten Jim Leighton in the Scots goal but somehow did. For a moment the revitalised Spaniards seemed capable of taking a point until Dalglish intervened with a meandering run across the penalty area and a blinding shot to the top corner of the net. In scoring he ensured a Scottish victory and equalled the tally of Denis Law who had also scored 30 goals for Scotland. The testimony of the Spanish coach, Munoz, must have been music to the ears of Stein: "It was a masterpiece of technique." Stein himself was in no doubt about the worth of the performance: "It was the most satisfactory game since I became manager of Scotland. We scored three goals against a quality team who came to defend." With two wins from two games it did not appear that qualifying for Mexico would present any great difficulty even allowing for the fact that not too much could be looked for from the return game against Spain.

Unsurprisingly, not too much was gained in Seville. Late on the night of 27 February 1985 Jock Stein gave an interview to Radio Clyde's Paul Cooney, in the immediate aftermath of a 1-0 defeat at the hands of Spain in Seville's Sanchez Pizjuan Stadium. It is among the hardest tasks faced by a manager, this necessity to respond to intense questioning in the minutes following the final whistle. On this occasion Stein's normal placidity deserted him and although his words may appear comparatively mild on paper, there was no mistaking the real rasp of anger in his voice. It was as though all the chicanery of Spanish-speaking teams throughout his career, all the skulduggery of Racing Club, Atletico Madrid and even on occasion Real themselves had eventually proved too much for him to stomach. After regretting that the Scots had required to make two late substitutions on the day of the match when Nicol and Dalglish withdrew, and taking care to exculpate their replacements, the dam burst and a torrent of bitter words gushed from him.

"I don't think we play under the intimidation that they do. There were four bottles thrown on that park, oranges have been thrown, the behaviour of the crowd is something else. I think something should be done, they shouldn't get away with it, they seem to get away with it each time. People say it's a great atmosphere, it's a hostile atmosphere.

"They're not nice people to play against, they're not nice people to be among, actually. They got away with murder compared to Celtic [who had recently been compelled to replay a European tie against Rapid Vienna because of crowd trouble at Parkhead]. Celtic did a lot less than them [Spain], it was a spectator there. Tonight a player deliberately punched and spat on Maurice Johnston three times. People just stand aside and say 'That's football!' They shouldn't get away with it whether they are Real Madrid, Barcelona or whatever they are. The game's supposed to be the same in every country. You know how the game was played in Glasgow, a good sporting game. We won that game. I'm not making excuses in losing because I think anyone could come to Spain and lose, but what I do say is, I like to lose and lose properly. We didn't lose properly the [sic] night, we lost because of intimidation."

There is no mistaking the intensity of feeling there but the SFA did not feel moved to make any official protest and in truth the Scots had played poorly. They lost only one goal, to Clos early in the second half but the Scottish front men were leaden and when the one real chance fell to the unmarked Archibald, he took an eternity to turn on the ball and the chance was gone. From the trackside Stein would certainly see more than those watching at home but the impression gained was not one of excessive crowd misbehaviour.

Not for the first time the manager's use of substitutes was called in question with Nicholas given but eight minutes to achieve what Archibald had failed to do in 82, and McStay who had left the Scots right flank very exposed in the first half, lasting well into the second before making way for the more confident Strachan. It was another to add to the long catalogue of Scottish failures on foreign territory but the margin of defeat was narrow and over the two games between the countries Scotland could reasonably claim to have come out ahead. Provided that the Scots did merely what was expected of them and defeated Wales and Iceland in their next two matches they would be going to Mexico in the summer of 1986.

But an unlooked-for defeat at the hands of Wales on 27 March 1985 made the task of getting to Mexico much more difficult and certainly rendered more hag-ridden the remaining few months of Stein's life. Gordon Strachan was not playing and this was a serious loss because Strachan had the unswerving conviction of his own ability which all truly great players must have. Some eyebrows were raised at the late appearance of Graeme Souness who had been promoting his book on the Terry Wogan show but Stein brushed all comment aside in his tersest manner: "I don't think the player is belittling us in any way. He has often come and gone for us in the past and it's only a matter of an hour and a half late in reporting."

As has been mentioned, Wales had two world-class players in Rush and Hughes and another in their goalkeeper Neville Southall but equally they had three or four players with Third Division backgrounds who would not remotely have been considered for the Scotland side. Their record at Hampden was anything but inspiring: 34 years had elapsed since last they won in Scotland. They were however a robust and physical side who had not come to Scotland to be intimidated. If there was intimidation about, they would play an active part.

Stein's strategy was sensible enough and concerned itself with cutting off supplies to Rush and Hughes. The Scottish midfield was non-existent however, the two Welshmen saw plenty of the ball and even when it wasn't about they did enough cannoning-off Miller and McLeish to ensure that the two defenders spent a bruising night. The winning goal came from a deadly shot from Rush, although Stein was almost certainly right in his assertion that Hughes had backed into McLeish seconds previously. The remainder of the match saw frenetic Scottish pressure but virtually no shots. Souness committed a horrendous foul on Peter Nicholas and was inordinately lucky only to be booked by a complaisant Belgian referee, M Ponnet. When the final whistle sounded Wales became only the third team, behind England and Poland ever to beat Scotland at Hampden in a World Cup tie.

Despite his comment about the Welsh goal, Stein did not attempt to deny that Wales had been the better side. He was extremely disappointed with the Scots performance: "We were very nervous, never ourselves. It was the kind of game we always thought it would be, hard, fierce and fair." The braver observers permitted themselves the wry aside that if it was exactly the kind of game that we thought it would be, how had we come to lose, but the bulk of the Scottish football public now felt that Mexico might just be beyond reach. They had seen all this before.

By any sane standards of appraisal Scotland were very likely to win the match against Iceland in Reykjavik on 27th May 1985. Climatic conditions might be difficult, although not so very different from those of a Scottish spring, and the standard of Icelandic football had certainly improved remarkably. Stein himself had given oblique witness to this in the signing of Johannes Edvaldsson, although this took place while he was temporarily absent from Parkhead. Several Icelandic players now played with top European clubs and it is worth remarking as an indicator of things to come, that in the Scottish side which played Spain in Seville there had been three players attached to European clubs, compared with a solitary Anglo-Scot.

In winning 1-0 the Scots were most assuredly fortune's children. Their

155

stumbling, halting play was as unfamiliar as the pale yellow jerseys they wore. They had gone into the match in good heart, buoyed by a home victory over England the previous weekend. European Cup commitments had deprived them of the entire Liverpool contingent so that ruled out Dalglish, Hansen and Nicol while the players from the other club in that city, Graeme Sharp and Andy Gray, were unable to travel with the rest of the party because of a rearranged Everton fixture and came out later.

They watched from the other end of the field as the grey-sweatered Jim Leighton kept Scotland in the game with some brave early saves. When the initial Icelandic impetus seemed to have spent itself, Graeme Souness provided it with a stimulus when he crudely fouled Sigi Jonsson. Stein, whose whole career had been a campaign to protect the ball player, lost a few friends with his emphasis on the time the referee took to book Souness. It was evident that Jonsson's injury was serious and the Scotland manager really might have reflected on his good fortune that Souness for the second game in succession had been allowed to remain on the field, although the booking meant that he would now miss the match with Wales in Cardiff.

Before half-time Leighton had given further proof of his worth by saving a penalty kick taken by the Icelandic captain, Thordarsson. It was not a particularly well-taken penalty but it was a fine save. Time after time the Icelandic forwards ripped the Scottish side apart and time after time their finishing was embarrassing. With five minutes to go, when it looked as if Scotland might hang on for an unmerited draw, Strachan got away on the right and at the far post the enigmatic Jim Bett showed the locals how to turn the half-chance to account. Nor was the match finished even then for Iceland swept to the Scottish penalty area and a cross found Gudlaugsson in the clear. He controlled the ball beautifully on his chest, a piece of skill which no more than three or four of the Scots could have emulated, looked up, measured his shot and struck it unerringly past the post. Minutes later the final whistle went and the collective gasps of relief from the Scottish dug-out were almost audible in Glasgow.

Success might have been undeserved, although in the strictest analysis the Icelanders had been too spendthrift to merit victory, but two points had been gained and if the confident Welsh could be held in Cardiff Stein would be guaranteed another last attempt on the World Cup itself.

THE MAN

17

EVERY MAN'S HAND — THE MEDIA MAN

IF, over the years, the besetting sin of Rangers was arrogance, that of Celtic might fairly be said to have been suspicion which at times bordered on paranoia. That the club had its ill-wishers from earliest times is incontrovertible and that some of those ill-wishers were in high places is equally certain. It is impossible to avoid the conclusion that Sir George G. Graham, secretary of the SFA, was quite simply anti-Celtic, that at times Harry Swan of Hibernian appeared hardly less so and that much of the broadcasting from BBC Scotland in the days when Peter Thomson fronted the *Sportsreel* programme was lacking in impartiality and objectivity. There had been rough decisions on-field. On the famous occasion of the Victory Cup semi-final replay with Rangers in 1946 several Celtic players formed the opinion that the referee, M. C. Dale, was in no condition to control any match. The 1970 Scottish Cup Final against Aberdeen is often cited as an instance when refereeing decisions consistently went against Celtic and crucially affected the result. The failure to take any action against M. C. Dale back in 1946 was contrasted starkly with the suspension for two months of referee James Callaghan for his failure to send off John Hughes of Celtic in a match in August 1969 against Rangers.

Yet every club since the inception of organised association football has smarted under the lash of injustice on-field and off. Celtic however felt that they had evidence to show that there were racial and religious overtones to their slings of fortune. This was a comforting but very dangerous piece of knowledge to have. It encouraged self-deception and the idea that every reverse encountered was the result of sharp practice or worse. It led to a collective state of mind in which an essentially warm-hearted and generous club too often appeared to be suspicious and unwelcoming.

At its worst this attitude was exemplified in Sir Robert Kelly's book, *Celtic*. Criticism of this must be muted by the awareness that Sir Robert was a dying man when he finished it but the tone of much of the book is deplorable. When it appeared, Celtic had been the undisputed leaders of Scottish football for six years and a simple recital of things accomplished would have impressed more than the constant harping note of complaint and victimisation.

159

In saying this, two things have to be remembered — Stein's very close links with Robert Kelly and the timing of his own arrival at Parkhead, a few short months before the long-drawn-out chapter of the flying of the flag of the Irish Republic. In articles and interviews, a phrase which Stein would use was "those who tried to put this club out of the game".

The club saw itself as Ishmael, with every man's hand against it, and it must be accounted one of Stein's major failures, perhaps his only major failure, that not only did he fail to rid Celtic of this pervasive resentment but appeared to succumb to it himself. This was doubly unfortunate in that he was uniquely qualified by his own background, still more by his own achievements, to turn away from the compulsive licking of old sores.

If Celtic had been intemperately and unfairly criticised before the Stein era, there was little that a rational man could have taken exception to thereafter. The cynical might object that journalists and broadcasters could hardly do anything else, Celtic were the best side in Europe in 1967 and the second best side in the world, but the matter went beyond that. Long after Celtic had passed their peak, from 1972 when they were no longer a force in Europe although still winning league titles, their coverage tended to be very favourable, to such an extent indeed that it masked what were real and growing deteriorations.

A good example of this capacity for the self-inflicted wound was the

Stein, watched by John Clark, Charlie Gallagher, Willie Wallace and Ronnie Simpson, examinesa clip taken from The Celtic Story *the film produced to commemorate the Lisbon victory of 1967.*

160

flight to Tbilisi for the match against Dinamo Kiev in January 1966. The version of events which gained universal currency then in Scotland is that the Russians constantly put obstructions in the way of Celtic for the second leg of the tie in Russia, Celtic having a comfortable 3-0 lead to defend from Parkhead. What happened was as follows:

At the end of December the Russians offered Celtic facilities for a charter flight to Moscow, with a connecting internal flight to Tbilisi, or a direct flight from London to Tbilisi by a Russian airliner. The match had been shifted from Kiev to Tbilisi for climatic reasons and Dinamo Kiev were the very first Russian side to take part in a major European competition.

Celtic had the right of it when they complained that they had not dictated to the Russians how they should come to Glasgow but when they made representations, the secretary of the SFA, Willie Allan, conveyed to them that UEFA thought the Russian proposals reasonable.

Celtic did not and after much bickering by long-distance telephone the match was postponed for a week. There was a lot to do on the home front and Stein's only comment was "We are disappointed in many ways that there will be no match next week, but we have now reached the stage where we are past thinking of it." A decision was taken to charter a plane from Aer Lingus and no arrangements proposed by the Russians could have worked out worse. Ireland and Russia did not maintain diplomatic relations at highest level and negotiations had to be carried on through their respective embassies in London. The Russians, it should be said, had come to Scotland on a normal chartered flight.

The return journey from Russia was a nightmare. A breakdown in catering arrangements at Tbilisi cost two hours, a malfunctioning instrument panel at Moscow three more. Freezing rain meant a diversion from Copenhagen to Stockholm and an overnight stop. The catalogue of error continued next morning when a burst valve could not be replaced and a substitute plane had to be diverted from Frankfurt by way of Brussels. More dead than alive, the Celtic party staggered off the plane at eight in the evening to learn that the fixture against Hearts was still on the following day.

There were precedents for this. Rangers and Hearts themselves had been instructed to play following late returns from Europe. Celtic saw it as an attempt to wrest the league from them. The official league view was that there was a public to be considered, two clubs involved, and that the inability of the carrier to cope remotely adequately was not sufficient reason to postpone the match which in the event Celtic, not surprisingly, lost.

The club had not, in fact asked the league for a postponement giving as the reason for not so doing the fact that they had recently twice protested unavailingly against a decision to stage a League Cup semi-final and its subsequent replay at Ibrox Stadium. This did not deter the manager from sounding off in the *Celtic View* of 2 February 1966. "If I thought that ever again Celtic players, officials and supporters were in danger of suffering the experience we had last week through our journey to Tbilisi in Georgia . . . I would without hesitation tell the authorities what to do with their competition."

It has to be said that there was a touch of bravado in taking the team out to Parkhead very late at night for a training session after such a disastrous trip. At the back of Stein's mind in not asking formally for a postponement may well have been the realisation that crowds tended to be very large in the aftermath of a successful venture into Europe. The very next season 43,000 would watch a Hibernian match after a Celtic win in Zurich and there were over 40,000 at the Hearts match in question.

In the west of Scotland credit for footballing objectivity is given extremely sparingly, principally because it is not widely regarded as a virtue. Stein astonished me on one occasion in the vestibule at Parkhead when in reproving me for a broadcast criticism of some facet of Celtic's play the previous week he said, "With your background, you should not be helping them." The "them" needed no identification. This was an odd remark to come from a man who was consistently good on the major issues.

In the 'Old Firm' rivalry he basically did not believe that there were any neutrals and it was this more than anything else which led him to aim for long-term superiority over Rangers. A reporter seen in the Ibrox hallway after Rangers had defeated Celtic was very likely to attract a snarled, "I might have known I would have seen *you* here!" There would be no long-term legacy of enmity but it was interesting and a little saddening to see that magnanimity in victory, far less in defeat, was rather long in coming.

For almost thirty years, against this background, Stein dominated, charmed, bullied and manipulated both the sporting press and the broadcasting media. He was abundantly and deservedly praised for his achievements and given a fairly easy ride over his last three or four years at Parkhead when it had become obvious that Celtic were a declining force. In this period the club consistently got a better press than its performances deserved in absolute terms.

Why was this? There were several reasons of varying degrees of importance. First and most telling, Stein's performance for much of his managerial career was so good as virtually to place him beyond criticism. The reporter who attempted to criticise was in grave danger of making himself look stupid, since even slight temporary aberrations could be followed swiftly by some magnificent coup or other. There was a tremendous risk involved in venturing to criticise one of the great managers of all time.

There was also a profound and genuine feeling of gratitude towards Stein from writers and broadcasters. In a sense his European exploits had made them important. He had certainly sold papers for them, made their views of interest to a European, indeed world, public and he had provided them without doubt with their most memorable and exciting sporting moments. Having lived for years in the scornful shadow of Fleet Street the Scottish pressmen and broadcasters would have been less than human had they felt no sense of gratitude towards their liberator.

Again, there was another sense in which Stein was a newspaperman's delight. He was eminently quotable and he understood the need for reporters to have something with which to satisfy an editor. Even when under contract to the *Sunday Mirror*, he played fair with the rest of the press corps and was adept at releasing small items of news in his own time and on his own terms.

On the surface at least he was convivial with newspapermen and broadcasters. Small talk came easily to him and in this he was significantly different from his great predecessors, Maley of Celtic and Struth, Symon and Waddell of Rangers. All the four named had been dour, uncommunicative, often overtly contemptuous of those who so arduously publicised them. The story told of Scot Symon, that when there was fog in the centre of Glasgow just before an important European match and an enterprising reporter telephoned Ibrox Park to find out if it was foggy out there he received the managerial reply — "No comment", could never have been told of Stein. The latter was a more overtly warm man and if he had any feelings of contempt for the press he very effectively disguised them.

That is not to say that he lived in perpetual amity with the newspaper world. The relationship was always tempestuous. He was a notable wrongfooter of the opposition. He had the habit of picking on an individual reporter in a crowded after-match room and identifying publicly some fairly amiable weaknesses. Always there was the unspoken suggestion that if he chose, he could identify some rather less amiable weaknesses. There was a general belief that in the same way as the press kept tabs on most managers, so Stein kept tabs on the press. In an intensely competitive profession there were often guiltily mixed feelings as journalists watched him pick off one of their number. Next week it would be their turn.

His losses of temper gave the impression, and it was a curious impression, of being slightly calculated — "I will lose my temper with *him*, now." He had the good teacher's trick of being able to convince his audience that he was furiously angry while with part of his mind he stood apart, watching himself behave thus.

He was indeed formidable when he was angry. He could be a

physically threatening presence. Even when not present, his bludgeoning manner could cause at least momentary consternation. There was the celebrated Radio Clyde broadcast at the end of season 1976-77 when having been congratulated on the regaining of the league championship he suddenly rounded on the two presenters, Richard Park and the author. For a torrid five minutes he accused the station of a biased approach towards Celtic Football Club and the writer at least found it more of a flustering experience than it should have been for someone with more than 20 years in broadcasting. Richard Park was referred to frequently as "Ibrox Park" and "Bob Crampsey has never liked us anyway".

He appeared to have an especial dislike of photographers which broke surface from time to time. In November 1966 Bobby Murdoch was sent from the field in a match against St Mirren and Stein physically stopped three photographers from recording the incident. He was quite unrepentant. "It's not right for a press photographer to get pictures of a player who has been ordered off." His sense of fairness and fitness was outraged; he was worried that a photographer at such a time might provoke a player to even greater misdemeanour.

There was another flare-up when Auld and Gemmell appeared back at Parkhead to have matters resolved after they had been sent home from the American tour of 1970. A photographer asked an apparently innocuous question and Stein rounded on him with an anger which seemed totally disproportionate. It was in tragic character that there should have been the altercation with another photographer at Cardiff a few minutes before his death.

He fiercely and lastingly resented anything he took to be unfair coverage and he had a broad definition of unfair coverage. Reference has already been made to his anger at the BBC televised coverage of the South American matches in 1967. That was BBC London but four years later their Glasgow counterparts were coming under the lash for failing to cover a friendly match in the city between Celtic and their conquerors in the 1970 European Cup Final, Feyenoord. Stein's comment was: "It doesn't surprise me. I have come to expect this sort of thing from the *Sportsreel* programme."

On such occasions his sense of humour could and did desert him. He over-reacted in a game against Dundee United in January 1966 to what had clearly been intended as a humorous aside with no malicious motive whatsoever: "It was surprising to read the comments of two experienced journalists, admittedly in supposedly jocular fashion, that the start, which was put back five minutes, should have been delayed by forty-five because the first half was in their opinion dull."

As with other top-rank managers, his press conferences tended to resemble audiences at the court of Henry VIII, the courtiers for the most part subservient and the main item of interest the discovery of those who were out of favour. To avoid this being too damaging to their cause, newspapers would sometimes arrange to have the really hard questions asked by the news, rather than sports, reporters so that if the questioning journalists were banished the scene it would not impede the flow of daily news from the ground.

There were times when he had absolutely legitimate grounds for complaint about what was written, especially in English newspapers or spoken in English broadcasts. Scots sports reporters were often stigmatised as fans with typewriters but few people are more chauvinistic and xenophobic than English sports commentators who in the course of transmission are apt to assume that the whole of Great Britain is hanging on an English victory. There are at least three nations within the British Isles which are not awaiting such an outcome from any match in which England are engaged.

The tradition of scathing comment in English newspapers to exasperate or stimulate Scottish readers is of ancient pedigree. When all allowance has been made for possible tongue in cheek, the following quotation from Bill Brown, London correspondent of the *Evening Times* is still breathtaking in its arrogance. It was written after the knighting of Sir Matt Busby and Brown delivered himself thus: "Some Scots may ask that if Sir Matt Busby has been knighted why not Jock Stein? Patience lads. Jock Stein is a veritable babe in arms in the football game, a manager of stripling standing compared with Busby. A hardy intelligent stripling, mind you. But give him room to develop, to show us all that his managership of Celtic is no flash in the pan of a few seasons but will last. Then we will be pleased to put his name before the Queen for the accolade."

Sad stuff, and perhaps it is barely worth mentioning that at this stage the "stripling" had won the European Cup and reached the final, won four successive league championships and taken the Scottish Cup with two different clubs. A substitution occurs to the reader of Brown's piece. "*WE* must see whether the feat of Sir Edmund Hillary is an isolated achievement or whether he will go on to climb other mountains."

In his early days at Dunfermline and again when he moved to Parkhead Jock Stein used the press brilliantly in a successful endeavour to remove rival clubs from the back pages of the newspapers. Thus when in the first few months of his taking up the Parkhead post he engaged several Brazilian players on a trial basis, he was careful to tell the press that he thought that he had a better than average player in one of them, Ayrton Inacio. In the event, the player came nowhere near making the top professional grade in Scotland but his coming had provided a talking-point. Reference had been made elsewhere to the tremendous boost he gave for the match against Zagreb shortly before the European Cup tie with Vojvodina. If it had any purpose at all it was to confuse the Yugoslavs about his intentions then but he secured the additional bonus

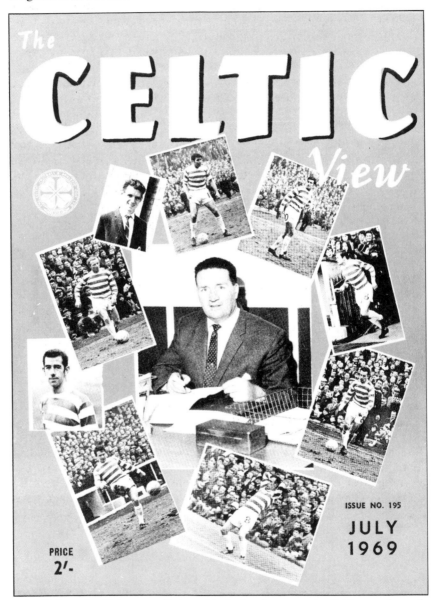

The Hub or the Universe — Stein at his desk, players on the field, crowds on the terracing.

of attracting a huge crowd to watch a friendly match in which a stated policy of all-out attack brought not a single goal against the Yugoslav side Zagreb.

He was not inclined to let any criticism pass unnoticed. In the aftermath of the League Cup Final of 1969 when St Johnstone lost a very early goal but recovered well to keep the margin to that goal, he had this to say: "I keep reading about St Johnstone's nervous start and the great Fallon saves in the second half but if we had taken our chances in the first 20 minutes there would not have been a second half."

His own newspaper column was of course ghosted but he wrote a weekly column for the *Celtic View* almost every week from the paper's inception in 1965 until October 1968 when the weekly deadline became too onerous. In his own performances on radio and television he was impressive and almost invariably value for money. If anything he was more suited to television because on radio his voice had a tendency to register as querulous to the listener who could not see the considering expression and often the half-smile which would have accompanied them on the screen.

Criticism was slow to build up even in his later and less spectacular years at Parkhead. Again, there were reasons for this, reasons by no means ignoble. Judgement had to be suspended in the light of the very serious car crash of 1975 when for a considerable time afterwards the day-to-day direction of the club was not in his hands. Again, just when it looked as if his touch had gone a Scottish Cup or League Cup would be won or a championship against the collar. There was a reluctance among reporters to believe that there was any diminution in ability and although some of the signings made in the middle 1970s held out little prospect of being successful, the assumption had to be that Stein knew what he was doing.

Eventually there came a widening recognition that what observers thought was happening was actually happening. In a thoughtful and well-reasoned article in the *Sunday Mail* on 6 November 1977 Allan Heron stated that "Now nobody fears Celtic". His assessment which time proved to err only on the side of optimism was that it would be five years before Celtic were a force in Europe again. Stein himself, on the morning after the match in Salzburg against Wacker Innsbruck in the European Cup, admitted that "It's going to be a long way back from this". Would Stein be given time for the journey? Even at this late date he had more to fear from within than from the sports journalists.

18

PLAYERS MAN?

IN building a picture of Stein as manager certain contradictions or apparent contradictions emerge. On the one hand there is the jocular man who chaffed and gagged with his players, on the other the stern disciplinarian whose word was law. This is perhaps because Jock Stein, although he was very good at small talk and enjoyed the camaraderie of football folk — indeed sparkled in such company — was not by nature an extrovert. There was always the feeling that his was not so much a contrived as a controlled sociability and this despite the fact that other managers such as Walter McCrae of Kilmarnock and John Greig of Rangers correctly identified his skill with words as one of the greatest of his managerial strengths.

He could certainly be stern and would brook no flouting of his authority. This was evidenced by his immediate and furious pursuit of Jimmy Johnstone in a league match at Parkhead when the little winger very publicly dissented from the decision to substitute him. He drove his players hard at training sessions and was keen that they should dress formally on any occasion on which they might be taken as representing their club, which was most of the time. He would not allow swearing although he swore himself, even if rather mildly and rarely in a public situation.

With his first two clubs, Dunfermline Athletic and Hibernian, his task was to give his players belief in themselves — in the Scots phrase, a "guid conceit of themselves". If Dunfermline were to emulate the 'Old Firm', even in the short term, then it was psychologically important that there should be a rig of the day in club blazer and flannels, that the team should stay at good hotels when they travelled and that they should play golf collectively at a good local course. Stein fought for, and secured, all these things.

With Hibernian the tradition and reputation was long established, the primary task was to convince his playing staff that they had the necessary ability. Stein was superb in this aspect of the job. His pre-match address to his troops before one of the three victories which they recorded over Rangers in that season was simply: "Our inside-forwards this afternoon are Hamilton and Quinn. Theirs are X and Y. The difference in class is enormous. Out you go and enjoy yourselves." They went and they did. With this went a canny realisation that players were often in trouble when they began to read and believe their press cuttings.

He did not let a player's reputation stand in the way of his decisions on team selection. Tommy Gemmell and Billy McNeill, at the height of their careers, both knew what it was like to look at the team sheet and find that their names were not on it. He normally abided by his own rule of not criticising players in public but occasionally departed from it if he thought a player's attitude or lack of self-confidence or generally unsatisfactory approach merited it.

Transfer of Power — One of the last photographs taken of Stein as a Celtic employee. He is flanked by Billy McNeill, his successor and the new second in command John Clark.

169

The elegant and hard-working Tom Callaghan took a disappointingly long time to settle at Parkhead and indeed was never really accepted by the bulk of the support, perhaps suffering from his own unselfishness. Stein tried to jolt him: "I told him, 'You were brought here because in my view you are a great player. You weren't brought to be nursed along, you're the ready-made article. Now get out there and force your talents on the game.'"

He was harder on Harry Hood, a more prolific scorer and a player with great skills and delicacy of touch but lacking, Stein felt, in endeavour on occasions: "He's made me angry, justifiably so, because I knew he had so much more to give us."

Skill which was unharnessed or wilfully tossed away was guaranteed to make him furious with the player in question. On the international front the casual approach of John Robertson, a player for whose ability he had a deep regard, provoked the following outburst at the World Cup of 1982: "If there's a slovenly way to do things he'll do it."

He flayed his own side collectively when effort had been lacking. After the League Cup Final of 1973 against Dundee, which because of the power cuts that then prevailed was played with a one o'clock kick-off, he described the Celtic performance as follows: "The pre-match atmosphere was unreal, the conditions were unreal and the form and attitude of the Celtic players were unreal. They apparently thought that they had just to appear on the field and victory would be accomplished. The scars left by this defeat will not heal quickly nor be easily forgotten. It was a dismal display."

Stein's anger on this occasion was perhaps understandable since the defeat meant that Celtic had lost no fewer than ten of the last 13 finals in which they had participated. The League Cup was a remarkably unsuccessful competition for him after the initial five in a row burst which heralded the start of his managerial career at Parkhead. Nine more visits to the final brought but one solitary success.

Stein was often to say that nothing in professional football gave him more pleasure than to see the boys become men through its medium, acquire wives and families and set up home in reasonable comfort. In wage negotiations, however, he very much favoured a system of lavish bonuses and comparatively low basic wages. This is a perfectly reasonable point of view since association football has got to be about incentives and too high a basic wage can leave players complacent and unambitious. As against this, a pay packet which depends for its weight on the caprices of footballing fortune is going to vary greatly. Not only will it be affected by results but injury, a recurrent hazard, could keep a player out of the first-team squad for months on end and deprive him of the chance of making the really large sums. Such a system was tilted in favour of the young player without family commitments and the fly-by-night.

He worked players hard in training and could adversely affect those of a retiring or nervous disposition. John Fallon could rarely capture in competitive matches the form which made him such a consistently brilliant goalkeeper in training. It always seemed that Stein never quite could bring himself to realise the special qualities which are required of a goalkeeper.

He was well aware that a very powerful part of the attraction of football for the supporter was nostalgia but he did not suffer himself to be sentimental where players were concerned. He helped to obtain good severance terms for such as Bobby Murdoch when the time came for him to move on to Middlesbrough but he was quick to realise when he could do no more with or for Jimmy Johnstone. The little winger was idolised by the support and there were many who would have argued for his retention but Stein could not let past glories stand in the way of present inconsistency. He had foreshadowed a possible parting at the end of May 1974: "Jimmy Johnstone will have to show more dedication if he is to be of any use to Celtic next season." Twelve months later, when the league championship had been lost for the first time in ten years, Stein had this to say: "I believe that Jimmy Johnstone has climbed all mountains possible with Celtic. He now needs a new challenge to inspire him."

It would be misleading to convey an impression of unremitting sternness. Sometimes he could almost be over-tender towards young players. A young goalkeeper, Graham Barclay, had been brought into the first team for a Scottish Cup tie against Clydebank in February 1975 and performed well enough in a 4-1 victory. He was left out for the following week's league match against Hibernian because, in Stein's judgement, it was not a game in which to put a young player's reputation at stake. From then until the end of his career Stein was to be notably more cautious in his introduction of young players at club and national level. It requires to be said, though, that however well intentioned the protection of Barclay, it might well have been taken by the young player as a vote of no confidence and in fact he was never to establish himself in the Celtic first team.

In general Jock Stein was supportive of young players. Danny McGrain found him to be especially good with those players on the fringe of the first team. It was Stein's practice to introduce a youngster, give him a few games and then return him to the reserves. He was punctilious in telling a player in such cases why he was doing this. McGrain had been a little puzzled since he thought he was doing well but Stein had detected a tendency for him to flag in the closing stages of a match and his purpose in temporarily dropping him was to work on his stamina.

At training or in matches he avoided rebuking young players, and the

171

new recruit learned what was expected of him indirectly, through listening to reproofs directed at such as Billy McNeill and Jimmy Johnstone. He was also absorbing the further lesson that if he himself attained star rating, that would not absolve him from experiencing a managerial tongue-lashing whenever Stein thought that he had incurred it.

Where it was necessary, he had endless reserves of patience. Danny McGrain recounts that when he was recovering from the injury which left him with a fractured skull, Stein himself supervised innumerable sessions at the training ground, Barrowfield. For hours he threw a plastic ball at him for him to head, gradually building up to the heading of a normal ball and then to heading under physical challenge.

In team talks and match preparations his general tactic was to build up the smaller teams and reassure his own players about the more powerful ones. When the club was playing away he would combine the bed-check round with individual visitation so that each player knew precisely what would be required of him. He did not allow his captain much if any tactical freedom and he did not welcome the "What if?" type of question in pre-match talks. He had made up his mind and he wanted no doubts or vacillations creeping in.

Stein was not a great praiser of players while they were within earshot, and, psychologist that he was, he would balance that by occasionally saying nothing at all in the way of reproof after some particularly sub-standard performance by the team. Ten years on it was absolutely automatic for Danny McGrain to talk invariably of "Mr Stein". He admits to only ever once having called him "Jock" — at his testimonial and the effort of doing so almost killed him.

Stein could and did join in some of the other activities of the players. The only other game which he genuinely liked was bowls, which not too many of the younger men played. He was a useful snooker player, although one of his first acts as manager at Parkhead had been to replace the billiard table with a table tennis one to sharpen reflexes. His own snooker ability was not so much a particular brilliance in his performance as a capacity for talking his opponent into going for extravagant shots. Gratifyingly often these failed to come off and left the ball poised above the pocket for Stein. He played golf with a detached vigour and a swing reminiscent of the Grim Reaper. It is hard to avoid the conclusion that he thought the chief virtue of the game was that it enabled a manager to supervise his charges in healthy surroundings.

Inevitably, his influence with the players weakened over the years. His Lisbon side had included players such as Chalmers, Clark, Murdoch, McNeill and Lennox who had been several seasons at Parkhead and had not known success. That changed with the arrival of

Stein, changed almost overnight, and the players naturally and correctly connected the two. At a later date, the Hays and Macaris came into a side which had not known failure so that the beginning of a return to non-success was that bit more disappointing. They became less prepared to sit out lengthy periods with the reserves in the hope that they might one day regain their first-team place. In his own phrase "Even if you're still right there comes a time when they've stopped listening to you".

With one category of player he was always profoundly uneasy. He found it difficult to comprehend players such as John Cushley and Jim Craig who had pursued successful careers outside of football. They were good players why did they want to be interested in anything else? There may have been the thought too that because of this they were less dependent on him than their less fortunate colleagues, and perhaps a certain fear of being verbally bested in public.

Almost to the end he had the amazing quality of inspiring confidence and belief in his players. It had to do with not compromising standards. Something he had said early on and would say again in June 1976 gave them a proper feeling of importance: "Celtic jerseys are not for second bests. It is the jersey worn by men like McNeill,' Tommy Gemmell, Clark, Auld, McBride and Chalmers. It won't shrink to fit an inferior player."

19

ESTABLISHING AN ASCENDANCY
— STEIN AND RANGERS

SINCE the end of the First World War Rangers had been indisputably the leading club in Scottish football. They were much better and therefore more consistently successful than any rival. They won more Scottish Cups and Scottish league championships than any other side, they supplied more players to the Scottish international team and they were by far the best-known Scottish club side in England and Europe. From time to time Motherwell might challenge fairly hard in the league, Celtic would win cups with moderate frequency and in the 1950s first Hibernian and later Hearts would hint at a sustained Edinburgh challenge. Such forays proved to be comparatively brief affairs and soon the normal state of things would again pertain and Rangers would resume their wonted supremacy.

It was this effortless and unquestioned superiority that Stein set himself to destroy. He had begun this process modestly at Dunfermline where under his guidance the Fife club secured their first-ever point at Ibrox and he had stepped up the pace when at Easter Road where in his year as manager Hibernian defeated the Ibrox club no fewer than three times, winning both league matches and dismissing Rangers from the Scottish Cup.

Stein was convinced that the greatest advantage which Rangers possessed was their reputation which was so overpowering that opponents played the legend and not the eleven Rangers players on the pitch that day. He was under no illusions about the magnitude of the task which he had set himself. Rangers were very much the Establishment club. In Glasgow coffee rooms of a Monday morning the business community was either discussing the performance of the Ibrox club or it was discussing Rugby Union football. It was taken for granted that Rangers would triumph, would prevail. It was the natural order of things.

At Parkhead, for the first time, Stein had the potential and the resources to mount a sustained challenge. He began by enlisting the aid of the press and to do that he had to make sure that the club was newsworthy. He was a never-failing source of copy. The last stand of the Lisbon Lions was a great story in itself but there were others, such as the time when every player appeared with the number eight on his shorts to celebrate the winning of an eighth consecutive league championship. That of course was much later and by then the objective had well nigh been achieved. In between times there had been the competition in the club newspaper, the *Celtic View* to design a change strip to the famous green and white hoops. Much publicity was given to the winning entry, green and black stripes, black shorts and green and black stockings and nobody seemed to notice when, after a couple of airings, the strip vanished into forgetfulness and the lumber cupboard. The important thing was that the man in charge now would comment, would talk to reporters. His predecessor, Jimmy McGrory, had been universally esteemed but he had been too nice a man to have the cutting edge that often provides the memorable quote. Reserve centre-half John Cushley recalls that as the Celtic team were taking the field, McGrory, pipe perpetually in mouth, would nod amiably and say, "Good day for shooting". Cushley's ambition was to stick in the first team long enough to see the arrival of the day which would not be a good one for shooting.

If Celtic were to become the ascendancy club then clearly Rangers would have to be overturned. Yet in order to do this Stein would have to take the pressure off his own players by playing down the exaggerated importance attached to 'Old Firm' games, particularly individual 'Old Firm' games. From his earliest days as Celtic manager he endeavoured to divert attention from clashes with Rangers by quoting European Cup successes. He was keenly conscious that many Celtic supporters did not remotely subscribe to this line of thinking and that a sizeable number would have been prepared to lose every other league game comparatively happily provided that the two against Rangers were won convincingly. Such a death or glory attitude was not particularly congenial to Stein and when he became international manager he saw one of his most pressing jobs as being to wean the Scottish supporter away from the notion that a win against England made up for total mediocrity against other opposition.

When all allowances have been made for its exaggeration in press reporting and in fiction, and bearing in mind that some acute people have realised that its exploitation is commercially profitable, there is still no doubt that the Celtic-Rangers rivalry has been a corrosive element in west of Scotland society. The cause may be genuine hatred or financial expediency or a mixture of both but it would be pointless and dishonest to minimise its importance. Stein was perfectly aware that he would be judged by what he did against his great traditional rivals and, almost despite himself, he peculiarly cherished such victories, took defeats particularly to heart and resented fiercely criticisms directed at him by his own supporters on such occasions. Examples abound and the following instances provide an insight to his thinking.

Early in September 1967 Celtic defeated Rangers 3-1 in a League Cup match at Parkhead which had been studded with controversial decisions, the bulk of which had gone against the home side. Writing in the *Celtic View* of 6 September 1967 Stein reflected on the match as follows: "It was the manner of our victory last Wednesday night and the fact that we won convincingly in circumstances which seemed so much against us and on an occasion on which lesser players than Celtic's might have become despondent long before the end that led me to speak so highly of our success. But when all the circumstances are taken into account, one win over Rangers does not compare with beating teams like Dinamo Kiev, Inter Milan and Real Madrid in Spain."

This was establishing rank order with a vengeance. What Stein was in effect saying was that "We are used to playing with the big boys and you [Rangers] are not." Even with a European Cup success behind him there was still a touch of effrontery about such a statement in 1967. This was pointed up by the result of the very next 'Old Firm' game, a 1-0 win for Rangers at Ibrox which drew the following observation from the Celtic manager: "Our run of success against Rangers has been good for us but has not been easily accepted elsewhere . . . we have to rethink our approach to the next 'Old Firm' game."

Almost brutally, he strove to foster the notion that Rangers were afraid of Celtic. In 1968 when Rangers withdrew from the Glasgow Cup, pleading congestion of fixtures, Stein in his official report used the bludgeoning phrase "In the Glasgow Cup we met and defeated all those clubs who were eligible for entry and who were prepared to play us." He was not above suggesting that the opposition were too physical whereas his own side were merely robust. Before an 'Old Firm' encounter of August 1968 and writing again in the *Celtic View* he declared: "Celtic fear no opponents but we do admit to preferring to play in a contest in which the rules are abided by on the field and outside of which the spectators exercise no unfair influence."

This match was duly played and won but in the jealous eyes of Stein, the wrong reasons had been attributed to the Celtic victory. "I am a little surprised to note how great an emphasis has been placed on the nature of the two Celtic goals at Ibrox. 'Gifts' they are described. I prefer to believe that Rangers were forced into error through their fear of the pace and purpose of our striking forwards, especially Lennox."

When in the following January, a visit to Ibrox was much less successful and he was heavily criticised for negative tactics in the 1-0 defeat by Rangers, he was clearly stung. "Fear of the opposition never enters my mind nor the minds of the Celtic players. Why should it when we of Celtic have played several teams of better quality than we can meet in Scotland nowadays and have not had the slightest fear of them?"

And, finally, when the great Scottish Cup final success of 1969 was criticised as having been a rough and dirty match Stein's riposte was simply this: "When we weigh everything up what could be more factual and satisfactory than to know that for all the bleating and wailing the Scottish Cup final score was Celtic 4 Rangers 0?"

He was, above all, anxious to establish Celtic not only as *the* Scottish team but as the *Scottish* team and the semantics are extremely important. It amused him that a side which was rightly proud of its early Irish connections should have won the supreme honour, the European Cup with eleven names — Simpson; Craig, Gemmell, Murdoch, McNeill, Clark, Johnstone, Wallace, Chalmers, Auld, Lennox — that could not have been more Scottish.

He was pleased and proud, as was club chairman Robert Kelly that the Moderator of the General Assembly of the Church of Scotland, the Rt. Rev. Dr W. Roy Sanderson had sent congratulations to Celtic Football Club on winning the European Cup in Lisbon and so adding greatly to the country's sporting prestige. He deeply appreciated the generous and courageous courtesy of Rangers' chairman John Lawrence in going to Abbotsinch Airport to welcome the returning Celtic party, an action which was by no means universally popular with the supporters of Mr. Lawrence's own club.

He was always, therefore, the more angry when Celtic followers misbehaved and it was such instances which caused him to dive into the terracing at Stirling in August 1972 to remonstrate forcibly with those misconducting themselves. He felt that such behaviour diminished Celtic's claim to be a national side, something in which he fiercely believed, having imbibed Robert Kelly's creed of "always pro-Celtic, always anti-nobody". When rebuked for putting himself in danger of loss of dignity if nothing worse, he retorted furiously, "It was something I've felt like doing for quite a while. The bad element . . . the wreckers . . . are singing and chanting about things which have nothing to do with football. Surely there are enough Celtic songs without introducing religion or politics or anything else."

It was this wish for a national dimension that caused him to launch an attack in the *Celtic View* of 8 August 1973 on a badly behaved section of the travelling support. "We don't want hooligans in our colours running riot through Dundee or Perth. We want trains going back in the same state that they came out." He knew that even in the early 1970s, a small section of the press might well judge Celtic supporters by harsher standards than they would apply elsewhere. He rejected absolutely the notion that both sets of supporters were equally culpable, almost certainly because he realised that had his own circumstances been different, nothing could have brought a young Catholic miner from Lanarkshire to manage at Ibrox Park.

His other aims where Rangers were concerned was to foster an altogether healthier rivalry between the clubs. He was especially anxious to eliminate crowd violence which he had come to see would drastically reduce attendances and perhaps end by driving the decently behaved spectator from the game. He was always prepared to try out innovations which might contribute towards this end and it was his own suggestion to stage a schoolboy match which would be played for 20 minutes each way at the *end* of an 'Old Firm' match. Celtic supporters were given a pressing invitation to stay behind and allow visiting Rangers fans time to disperse.

It looked as though the melancholy circumstances of the Ibrox Disaster of January 1971 might afford the opportunity for a lasting change in relationships. On 2 January 1971 an 'Old Firm' game had been played in a particularly sporting spirit before a remarkably well-behaved crowd. By great misfortune, both sides scored in the last minute, Celtic first and then Rangers in the dying seconds. At Celtic's goal, thousands of Rangers supporters had turned from the ground only to be recalled by the jubilant shouts seconds later. As they attempted to climb up the stairway to the terracings again they were engulfed in a wave of descending supporters. When the crushing and the pile-up stopped 66 people were dead and 145 lay injured. Both managers had helped to carry stretchers to the dressing-rooms which were pressed into service as casualty stations. Both sides attended a Requiem Mass in St. Andrew's RC Cathedral, Glasgow, three days later at which the readings were given by the Celtic full-back, Jim Craig, and the author. An Ibrox Disaster Fund was set up to which Celtic contributed £10,000 and there is no doubt that the immediate personal experience affected Stein very deeply. He reflected sadly on events: "The game had been played out in the most sporting manner and the players' good behaviour was reflected on the terracings. Surely this terrible tragedy must help to curb the bitterness and the bigotry of 'Old Firm' matches. When human life is at stake, as it was after the barrier crashed, then bigotry and bitterness seem sordid little things."

The amelioration was temporary and as an odd sidelight on preoccupations, most of the letters to the *Glasgow Herald* in the days which immediately followed concerned themselves with a previous Ibrox Disaster and whether on that day the accident had taken place in the North West or the South West section of the ground and whether the position of outside-left in the Scottish team had been filled by Bobby Templeton or Alec Smith.

Stein had considerable respect for his laconic self-effacing opposite number, Scot Symon of Rangers, but it was the constant and ostentatious successes of Stein which were to lead to the panic-stricken decision by Rangers to dispense with the services of Symon. Stein, having problems of his own at the time in South America, took time to send his fellow manager a telegram of regret. He had often twitted indirectly the manager of a Scottish side who filled it with Scandinavians and Germans — Thorolf Beck, Kaj Johansen, Jorn Sorensen, Erik Sorensen, Orjan Persson and Gerhard Neef all played at Ibrox about this time — but he had a profound regard for a fellow professional.

Having removed the experienced and shrewd Symon, the Rangers Board was flustered into further defensive reactions and ill-considered moves. As league championship followed league championship to Parkhead Rangers attempted to alter events by expensive signings such as Alex Ferguson, Andy Penman, Colin Stein, Quentin Young and the two Smiths, Dave and Alec, few of whom made any lasting impact.

A Public Relations Officer, Willie Allison, was appointed for what seemed to be no better reason than that Celtic had one in Jimmy McGrory and the parallel became exact when Allison was equally denied authority to say anything meaningful on behalf of the club. Rangers broke with tradition by going outside the club for a manager when they appointed the youthful David White of Clyde and then dismissed him when he was doing well by any reasonable standards. The reserve team at Ibrox filled up with experienced players who lost their edge and took places which effectively prevented a new generation coming through. A posse of dissaffected players went south — Jim Baxter, Ralph Brand, Colin Stein, Willie Johnstone — and their replacements were not of the same calibre. It is true to say that five or six years on, Jock Stein would have to admit that he no more than any other could keep a pool of players happy once matches and titles began to slip away.

The essential thing is that Stein came to obsess the Ibrox thinking and even considerable Rangers achievements such as the winning of the European Cup Winners' Cup in 1972 and the Premier League successes of 1975 and 1977 came to appear mere interruptions, slight obstacles to Celtic's triumphal progress and did not re-establish Rangers on the commanding heights of the Scottish football scene.

He was extremely objective about Rangers' players during his two spells as national manager. He recognised the brilliance of Willie Henderson and the marvellous professional approach and willingness to battle in lost causes of John Greig. He admired, too, the latter's inspirational capacity to turn a game not so much by personal brilliance as by personal example. Literally the last decision of Stein's life was to bring on a Rangers player as substitute at Cardiff, the gifted Davy Cooper whose enormous talent and flair for the big occasion were bound to commend themselves to him. How well Cooper repaid that call is recorded elsewhere.

That Stein succeeded in what he set out to do is beyond question. For a decade he identified major European competition with Celtic and when at last the sceptre fell from his grasp the new aspirant to the throne was not to be found across the city of Glasgow but far off to the north-east.

20

THE PINNACLE OF THE PROFESSION

IN *The Scottish Footballer* I attempted to describe the qualities and abilities which the ideal manager should have. These are not exclusively estimable human qualities. The meek may very well inherit the earth but they do not win European Cups or league championships.

Success in football managership is easy to quantify but less easy to describe. The mind automatically goes to the tally of league flags and cups won, but real success for Jock Stein at Dunfermline was keeping the club in the old-style First Division. There are those who would deny that there is any particular art or skill in football managership since the 'manufacturing process' — the winning of matches — is outside the direct physical control of the manager. Where however we see one man being successful with different clubs as Herbert Chapman, Eddie Turnbull and Jock Stein were, then the common factor, the man himself, will repay scrutiny. Stein's record more than stands comparison with the work of Herbert Chapman at Huddersfield and Arsenal and with that of Turnbull at Queen's Park, Aberdeen and Hibernian.

What would we find in the job description of our ideal manager? To his players he must be psychologist and master tactician, and he is looking for a few early strokes of luck to establish a temporary reputation and buy himself time. On his own admission Stein had this luck early on but the tactical knowledge was overpowering. In the last hour of his life he resisted the obvious substitution at Cardiff. He took off Gordon Strachan when there were more pressing candidates for removal and replaced him not with the battering-ram choice of Andy Gray but with the mercurial Davie Cooper who was not always a good risk. In the event Cooper reduced the Welsh defence to shreds and if the penalty which brought the equaliser was certainly fortunate, Napoleon's definition comes again to mind, "Luck is the residuum of good planning."

The great manager must be a good judge of a player and, with the exception of goalkeepers, a noted exception, Stein was certainly that. For all his hours of work with.goalkeepers it is difficult to avoid the conclusion when one looks at the long and basically ill-chosen list of keepers whom he brought to Parkhead that this most specialised of positions defeated and baffled him. Bobby Wraith, Gordon Marshall, Geir Karlssen, Denis Connachan, Alistair Hunter, none proved to be the answer. Asked to redesign the game from scratch he might well have opted to do without goalkeepers entirely.

Such a manager has to be a good judge of a scout, with sufficient faith in the latter to sign a player whom he himself has not seen if need be. He will be judged by how he handles the difficult players that he inherits and how wisely he resists the urge to sign those players that other managers could not handle — the ultimate temptation and folly of the trade. Stein certainly kept Jimmy Johnstone in the game where almost anyone else would have failed and he would go to endless trouble for the gifted footballer. Once on the platform at Edinburgh's Waverley Station I watched the tea-time rush hour boil and eddy round him as he awaited the Glasgow train and Willie Hamilton. A curt word and the player was bundled into a waiting taxi which swept him straight to Easter Road. In Stein's eyes, this was worthwhile. The difficult players are always by definition great players. Untalented troublemakers simply disappear.

In modern football the manager has a public relations job to do for his club and in this field alone Stein more than earned his salary. He was the Phineas T. Barnum of Scottish football and some of his more spectacular exploits thrill and delight 20 years on. He was determined that Celtic would monopolise the headlines, by good results wherever possible, but when these were not to hand there were other ways. There was the frenetic build-up to the friendly match with Dinamo Zagreb in 1967. This was a perfectly ordinary friendly match but under Stein's skilful massaging of the press it assumed galactic proportions. Celtic would use the game to try out a non-stop totally committed system of attack for the entire 90 minutes. A large crowd turned out on a winter's night, perhaps expecting to see a 1-1-9 formation. Whatever the thinking, and it was obscure, it did not work. Celtic lost 1-0 but the headlines and the gate receipts were there to testify to the excellence of the sales promotion.

The same flair decided that the Lisbon Lions would have one last glorious reunion in an otherwise meaningless end of season game against Clyde at Parkhead. A dead game became an event to cherish as the great side bade farewell in the grand manner. One of the recurrent myths which surround Stein is that he determined on the field at Lisbon that he would preserve the mystique of that particular side by never fielding those eleven players again, that they might remain unbeaten for evermore. This is not true. The Lisbon Lions made several subsequent appearances but on that afternoon against Clyde, Ronnie Simpson contented himself with parading in playing kit and taking a bow.

People in the entertainment world would have talked of *schmaltz* but Stein was an unashamed romantic and well knew the virtue of sentiment in football. He was quick to realise the Scots admiration for things Brazilian after the World Cups of 1958 and 1962 and although none of the Brazilian trialists that he brought to Parkhead soon after his arrival came anywhere near the league side, he had created interest, he had got the supporters talking. In doing this, he had delighted the press, his relations with which are discussed more fully elsewhere.

In football management men with very limited administrative experience are called on almost immediately to exercise diplomatic skills of a high nature in relation to their board of directors. The manager must be quick to realise where power lies within the board and ally himself thereto. Alternately he must achieve such a record of success as almost to defy dismissal. Stein had the total trust and confidence of Sir Robert Kelly and things were never quite so confident or unchallenged after the latter's death. There was a genuine respect between Stein and Desmond White but it was respect rather than any great warmth. In the end, not even the unique achievements of the manager could contrive a happy ending to his years at Parkhead.

We are so accustomed to the manager of a present-day football club having been a prominent player himself that it can easily be forgotten that this was not always the case. Such highly successful managers as Herbert Chapman of Huddersfield Town and Arsenal, Bill Struth of Rangers and Willie McCartney of Heart of Midlothian and Hibernian had either played no football at all at top level or so little that it hardly counted, but the advent of the modern track-suited manager changed things drastically. Stein had done just enough as a player to be able to ward off the "What did you do in the war, Daddy?" line of attack. He had a league and cup medal and he had been picked for the Scottish League against the Football League. It was not a lot but for most of his career it was enough, though always a potential source of weakness when he came to handle international sides.

There is no reason, save one, why non-footballers should not make perfectly effective managers but that reason is crucial. Players tend to despise those connected with the game who have not been exposed to the pressures of top-class football and it is hard for a manager who has never earned his living as a player to command the respect of his playing staff. Stein by his lavish use of bonuses had the reputation of being a players man, although the truth is of course that a manager must also be a salaried employee with an overriding responsibility to his Board of Directors.

There are quite a few managers who would pass with distinction in each of the areas indicated above. What then made Jock Stein so very special.

Above all, constantly and genuinely, he cared about the fans. There was no shadow of pretence in this. "A game without a crowd is nothing" was his credo. He left Dunfermline because the crowds would not come and he left Hibernian to work before bigger crowds. He desperately wanted to provide his followers not just with victory but with victory achieved in the grand manner. It was the failure to do this in Milan, failure even to lose in the grand manner that was so corrosive of his soul. Even in the great year of 1967, he was bitterly ashamed of the 90 minutes "kick it anywhere" which characterised the return match in Czechoslovakia against Dukla Prague. Bob Kelly had left him in no doubt of what *his* feelings were on the matter and while Stein was prepared to plead expediency, he saw the scintillating display in the Lisbon final not only as triumph but as atonement. For five years, Celtic were to be flamboyant, captivating and enchanting as they swept their stylish way to almost unrelieved success.

His greatest achievements were accomplished with home-grown resources and no huge transfer fees. Stein had a deep suspicion of and revulsion for expensive importations. "How many players are worth £250,000? How many will put six or seven thousand on the gate every Saturday?" Bill Shankly was more bombastic, but Jock Stein was no less fervid a patriot. Although it was Bob Kelly who made the remark about the pride he derived in winning a European trophy with 11 native-born Scots, the sentiments reflected those of the manager. He did not at all subscribe to the Scandinavian invasion of Scotland which was then at its height. He doubted the long-term commitment of such players and worried that information would be carried from the ground to their compatriots at rival clubs. His one venture in this direction he frankly regarded as a mistake.

For much of his career his depreciators, mostly in England, played down his victories, claiming that there were only two sides in Scottish football anyway and given that one of them, Rangers, was recruiting from a restricted field, the other should be the more successful. It is certainly true that during the 1970s Rangers' unwillingness to sign Catholics left them more and more dangerously exposed. There were two Catholic schoolboys in the Under-18 schoolboy international against England in 1955 and none at all the following year. In 1960 there were five and the following year six. Success at schoolboy level is not a very accurate predictor for the professional game but the point was that more than half the national side would never be available to Rangers, even to fail. Stein was often said to have declared that given two players of equal ability, one Catholic and the other not, he would sign the non-Catholic for by doing so he would remove two players from Rangers' planning. This dictum of Stein's should be taken with reservation: it is doubtful given the background of Celtic that he could have implemented it on any large scale and he was much more likely to have thought it than articulated it. Again the point that mattered was that Celtic had had this "advantage" long before Stein arrived and singularly failed to make use of it.

In winning nine consecutive league titles he used almost three different elevens. He performed prodigies in keeping the fringe players happy most of the time. No manager does it all the time and such as John Cushley preferred to light out for England rather than play in permanent reserve to Billy McNeill. With the eventual fall-off in performance came the inevitable discontent.

No more than any human being was he always right. Pride stood in the way of the sensible decision in Argentina and Celtic paid a heavy price in reputation for the untypical action of Sir Robert Kelly in allowing himself to be overruled. Stein was slow to see the potential danger of crowds encroaching on pitches. At first he regarded it as simply a tedious interruption for purposes of congratulating players. The author's view that spectators should not be on the pitch anywhere, anytime, in any circumstances struck no initial chord with him. Typically he came to restore order to the terracings by direct intervention at Stirling and other places, intervention which was dramatic but risky.

On the really big issues he was wise and compassionate. He was at his best when encouraging Paul Wilson to withstand the racist abuse to which he was subjected. He was nothing like as severe a disciplinarian as Struth or Maley and he not infrequently used the unexpected word "permissive" to describe his method of operation. His description of himself as someone who had to appear hard because at base he was a "big soft-hearted old miner" was not entirely true but neither was it fantasy. He shed tears when told of the extent of Brian McLaughlin's injury murmuring, "All that talent gone. What a waste!"

He very rarely subordinated entertainment to mere success and it was a genuine regret to him that others in the game were less generous of approach. His sides provided unforgettable moments of skill. He showed that attack *could* pay and he broke, at least for the moment, the essentially cowardly system of the Italians. He may not have known the poem — and that is not an assumption to make too confidently — but he certainly would have approved of the lines written by the Marquis of Montrose back in the seventeenth century:

> *He either fears his fate too much*
> *Or his deserts are small*
> *Who dares not put it to the touch*
> *To win or lose it all.*

As much as man can, he gave the impression of being in control of his own destiny. His record of achievement was imposing. Twice in his managerial career he led a Scottish club to victory over an English one in European matches played on a home and home basis. Almost by his own efforts he shifted the focus of European football attention to Glasgow for the better part of a decade.

It is doubtful if he ever uttered a dull sentence in his footballing life. On one occasion he felt aggrieved by decisions given by referee David Syme. As the latter came up the tunnel at the end of the game expecting the worst, the gigantic figure merely muttered, "Well done, son". As the bemused referee moved away came the follow-up. "Your father would have been proud of you." The reference was to David Syme's father Willie, also a Grade I referee who had, in Stein's eyes been equally hard on Celtic.

In his single-mindedness of purpose and the breadth of his knowledge he was more professional than anyone before or since. Musicians sometimes are quoted as saying: "There is Beethoven and then there are all the rest." It is very rare to look at any walk of life and to be able to say with certainty of one man, "He was the greatest of all". Quite simply, that is what Jock Stein was.

21

THE LONG LOOK BACK

ON 2 May 1985, the author of this book conducted an extensive on-stage interview with Jock Stein in the Carnegie Hall in Dunfermline. The occasion formed part of the memorial celebrations of the 150th anniversary of the birth of the town's famous philanthropist, Andrew Carnegie, and Stein used it mainly to look back, but with a glance towards Mexico at the very end of the evening.

It was a very typical Stein performance. There was the arrival barely five minutes before curtain-up, though such arrivals were neither designed to worry promoters or heighten an entrance. They merely reflected a judicious use of time. He appeared unobtrusively from a back corridor, apologising for having been detained by a family funeral. He did not particularly want to know where the areas of questioning would be. There was the confidence that he could deal with anything whatsoever that he might be asked, and in this confidence there was a simplicity that was genuine and curiously moving.

His pleasure at being back in Dunfermline was unfeigned. He had an abiding sense of gratitude to the club and, by extension, the town which had given him his first managerial opportunity in football. Since he had given Dunfermline its greatest-ever sporting moments, indeed brought it possibly more international renown than anyone save Carnegie himself, this affection was abundantly returned by the audience that night.

The proceedings started, inevitably, with a showing of the Scottish Cup Final replay of 1961 in which Dunfermline Athletic defeated Celtic 2-0. The massive head nodded, a quarter of a century later, in appreciation of the incredible goalkeeping of Eddie Connachan. There was a wry grimace of sympathy as the goalkeeper at the other end, the sanguine Frank Haffey, made the capital error which allowed Dunfermline to score the second and clinching goal.

The next film aroused his enthusiasm to an even greater degree for there on the screen in grainy black and white his Dunfermline side were retrieving a four-goal deficit against the Spanish club Valencia, one of the major sides of Europe. Having lost the first game 4-0 in Spain, the players had been induced by Stein to believe that the tie was not beyond redemption and in winning 6-2 at East End Park they forced a third though ultimately unsuccessful match.

In any subsequent questioning, one of his most marked characteristics emerged early on, what might be called a frank reserve, a very real contradiction. For the second Valencia match he had very daringly introduced Alex Edwards and Jackie Sinclair, two forwards who were 16 and 19 years old respectively. Edwards was a prodigious talent of uncertain temper. He should have been a fixture in the Scottish team but was never capped. To the suggestion that he must have been one of Stein's greatest disappointments there came the mild response that "maybe the boy got in with some people who advised him wrongly". Nothing more.

He did admit to applying pressure to the Portuguese referee on the night of the second Valencia match to ensure that the match went on although the frosty surface was barely playable. "Clearly it was our best chance against them. In some ways they were the more gifted side."

The main themes of the evening were appropriately Dunfermline and Scotland, but from time to time we wandered into other areas, with broadcasting coming under fire. Radio Clyde came in for particular criticism. How, he wondered, could a disc jockey front a sports programme? The fact that the "disc jockey" in question, Richard Park, has a wide and detailed knowledge of various sports did not mollify Stein in the slightest. How, he wondered again, could a listener phone in one week with a question and be on the programme the next week as a contributor? This was Stein at his outrageous baiting best as the listener referred to was Jim Craig, who on the twin grounds of his having been a member of the Lisbon European Cup team of 1967 and being fluently analytical in discussing football, might well have been thought by most to be worth a place on a sports programme.

It was a demonstration of his inherent ambivalence towards the media and the audience loved it. What sort of way was this, he demanded finally, to choose sports commentators? The only possible answer to give him was that it was exactly the method used for appointing football managers. Because 'A' had been highly successful as a player with club 'B', club 'C' offered him a job as manager. Even more bizarre, sometimes the offer came from his own club, 'B'.

I ventured to say to Jock that when he himself was appointed to Dunfermline there was no possible way of knowing that he would make even an adequate manager, far less a great one. Nor had Bill Struth or Herbert Chapman been players of any account. He thought about this and in a grudging tone, belied by a half-smile, muttered that there might just be something in that.

His loathing of the sectarian overtones which have disfigured Scottish football for so long surfaced when he recalled his interview for the

Dunfermline job. At an early stage during that meeting he was asked a question which he took to be an attempt to draw out a religious allegiance. His immediate reaction was to inform the Board that if that aspect was at all important to the directors then they were most certainly interviewing the wrong candidate.

On his reasons for eventually leaving East End Park: "There is always a time to move on." Always? Why did he not move south in 1970 when the offer was there? "That was loyalty, perhaps misplaced loyalty," he said without any marked bitterness.

He would not be drawn on the decision to move to Hibernian in 1964 rather than on the first offer from that club two years earlier. It seems very likely that the chief reason was his judgment that he was more likely to be given his head at Easter Road by the 1964 chairman, Bill Harrower, than by the latter's predecessor, Harry Swan. Stein in my hearing had rebuffed Swan's casual remark to him about having a job available with a brutally jovial, "Needin' an office boy then, Harry?" He had had the rare experience of being a genuine supremo in his first managerial job and he was subsequently unfitted for any subordinate role.

He had to a remarkable degree the habit of command, a command moreover which far exceeded simple ramrod authoritarianism and contained a great deal of flexibility. Even so, he became irked by the emphasis on managers: "I'd far rather talk about players. They're the ones who make things happen" — although he was much too intelligent wholly to believe this. It begged the question of why, with the same players often, things had not happened before his arrival at East End Park, Easter Road or Celtic Park.

He talked at length of those players who had delighted him, mainly his own. For the blazing ability and courage of Jimmy Johnstone his admiration was profound. He spoke affectionately of those two model professionals, Steve Chalmers and Bobby Lennox, of the commanding Billy McNeill, of the unflustered, undervalued John Clark who, unknown to him at that point, was in the audience.

There was regret for the players who had "got away" for one reason or another, for John Lunn of Dunfermline, dead of leukaemia in his twenties, for Alex Edwards, never the force he should have been, and above all for the prodigious talent of Willie Hamilton, both with Heart of Midlothian and Hibernian. Almost the only occasion on which I ever earned the big man's unqualified approval was when on a sports panel with him, I ventured the opinion that Willie Hamilton was the most visionary player I had seen in Scotland since World War Two.

He good-humouredly indicated that I was overdoing my advocacy of Charlie Gallagher and Harry Hood, two invaluable if rather marginal players during the nine championship years of Celtic: "You always liked them, Bob. You wouldn't win a championship with eleven Harry Hoods or Charlie Gallaghers!" I responded, "But you wouldn't win one without at least two of them in your side?" He replied, "True enough. It's getting the mix."

We switched to the position of the Scotland side, then struggling to qualify for Mexico. At that stage Scotland had recently lost to Wales at Hampden and had difficult away matches in prospect with Iceland and Wales. He appeared anxious, severely anxious, to damp down the audience here. He clearly wished to discourage any unreasonable expectations. He had tempered national enthusiasm in the run-up to Spain in 1982 and clearly, if he could help it, there would be no recurrence of the ludicrous euphoria which characterised the weeks before the departure for Argentina in 1978: "After all, we're a small country. The Finns and Norwegians, you don't get them saying they'll win the World Cup."

He thought that we could qualify although it would be hard. Once there he hoped that we performed to the best of our ability, that the travelling Scots supporters enjoyed the occasion, and, a significant phrase, "did not let themselves down". Not Scotland, not him, but themselves.

How did he see his own future? He thought that after Mexico, win or lose, he might well have had enough — but another wry flash — "Other people might be involved in that decision." It had been a marvellous experience, football, and he was eternally grateful for what it had done for him. There were no specific regrets. The earlier phrase "perhaps misplaced loyalty" was left to hang in the air. He finished by extending the hope that on the following Saturday Dunfermline Athletic would win their last match and so regain First Division status.

He had been on stage for much more than two hours and as Scotland's manager he must have had an infinity of things to do, yet he autographed every piece of paper that was thrust in front of him. He signed with a pleasant word and without affectation, detaching himself ruthlessly from bores and throwing a final jocular word to his old player, John Clark, who had come over from neighbouring Cowdenbeath.

In the car park, when everyone had gone, he spared ten minutes for Pat Woods who wanted one or two things cleared up for the history of Celtic which he was co-authoring. Again came the mixture of frankness and reserve: "I can't say anything about that particular topic just now, Pat. I might want to set it all down some day myself. You know how it is."

A few casual remarks on the success of the evening and the massive figure — it was a constant surprise how BIG he was — hirpled to his car and drove away into the late spring night.

MILESTONES IN THE CAREER OF JOCK STEIN

1922 Born 5 October at Burnbank, Hamilton, in Lanarkshire. Only son of George and Jane Stein.

1937 Leaves Greenfield School, Burnbank, and after a brief period in a carpet factory becomes a miner.

1942 Becomes signed senior footballer with Albion Rovers FC.

1950 Signs for Welsh non-league club, LLanelly Town.

1951 Signs for Celtic in December 1951, becomes full-time professional footballer and eventually club captain.

1954 Celtic win League and Cup double under his captaincy.

1956 Injury compels his retirement from football. Given job with Celtic coaching young players on staff.

1960 Takes over as manager of Dunfermline Athletic on 14 March.

1961 Under his leadership Dunfermline Athletic win Scottish Cup for the first time in their career.

1962 Dunfermline perform superbly in Europe, defeating Everton and forcing Valencia to a third game in the Inter Cities Fairs Cup after retrieving a four-goal deficit.

1964 In April Stein becomes manager of Hibernian FC. Within months of his arrival the club wins the Summer Cup.

1965 In March Stein becomes manager of Celtic FC. Within six weeks of arrival the club wins the Scottish Cup.

1966 Celtic win the league for the first time since 1954. They will win it again for the next eight years.

1967 Celtic win every competition for which they enter — League Cup, Scottish Cup, Glasgow Cup, Scottish League and European Cup, the first British side ever to win the last-named trophy.

1970 Celtic again reach the final of the European Cup but are defeated by Feyenoord of Holland. Stein linked with Manchester United.

Stein is awarded C.B.E. in Honour's List.

1975 Stein severely injured in car crash while returning from holiday. Effectively out of football for an entire season.

1977 Celtic win Premier League championship, Stein's tenth league title while with the club.

1978 Testimonial match at Celtic Park against Liverpool.

1978 Stein resigns as Celtic manager. Is offered and accepts, position on the Board with responsibility for fund-raising.

1978 Within weeks Stein resigns from the Board and accepts managership of Leeds United. Remains at Elland Road for less than two months.

1978 Accepts post of Scottish national team manager following the resignation of Alistair McLeod. Declares his long-term object will be to qualify for World Cups.

1982 Scottish side qualifies for World Cup in Spain and performs reasonably well against New Zealand, Brazil and Russia.

1985 Died at Ninian Park, Cardiff, on evening of 10 September as Scotland secured the point against Wales which made it virtually certain that they would qualify for the World Cup Finals in 1986 in Mexico.